The Unwelcome One

THE UNWELCOME ONE

ONE

Returning Home from Auschwitz

HANS FRANKENTHAL

In collaboration with Andreas Plake,
Babette Quinkert, and Florian Schmaltz
Translated from the German by John A. Broadwin

NORTHWESTERN UNIVERSITY PRESS
Evanston, Illinois

Northwestern University Press
Evanston, Illinois 60208-4210

Originally published in German in 1999 under the title *Verweigerte Rüeckkehr*. English translation copyright © 2002 by Northwestern University Press. Published 2002. All rights reserved.

Printed in the United States of America

10 9 8 7 6 5 4 3 2 1

ISBN 0-8101-1852-1 (cloth)
ISBN 0-8101-1887-4 (paper)

Library of Congress Cataloging-in-Publication Data

Frankenthal, Hans.
The unwelcome one : lessons learned after the Holocaust /
Hans Frankenthal ; in collaboration with Andreas Plake, Babette
Quinkert, and Florian Schmalz ; translated from the German by
John A. Broadwin.
p. cm.
ISBN 0-8101-1852-1 (alk. cloth) — ISBN 0-8101-1887-4
(paper : alk. paper)
1. Frankenthal, Hans. 2. Jews—Germany—Schmallenberg
—Biography. 3. Holocaust, Jewish (1939–1945)—Germany
—Schmallenberg—Personal narratives. 4. Schmallenberg (Ger-
many)—Biography. I. Plake, Andreas, 1957– . II. Quinkert,
Babette. III. Schmaltz, Florian. IV. Title.
DS135.G5F5865 2002
943′.226—dc21
2001006688

❖

Contents

Acknowledgments

We wish to express our heartfelt thanks to the many people who helped make this book a reality. In particular, we would like to acknowledge the following persons. Susanne Willems not only encouraged and advised us at every stage of the project, she also wrote several of the entries for the glossary. Dr. Irmtrud Wojak of the Fritz Bauer Institute in Frankfurt am Main helped us research the history of the Auschwitz trial. Peter Widmann of the Center for Research on Anti-Semitism's archives at the Technical University of Berlin gave us access to the Center's collection on the U.S. tribunal dealing with I. G. Farben executives (Case 6) that took place in Nuremberg after the war. We would also like to express our sincere gratitude to Dr. Gudrun Hentges, Mark Holzberger, Inge Junginger, and Professor Dr. Jürgen Schutte for making a number of suggestions and for taking the time to make corrections and improve the quality of the manuscript.

Babette Quinkert, Andreas Plake, and Florian Schmaltz

Biographical Note to German Edition

By the time Hans Frankenthal returned to his hometown of Schmallenberg in 1945 at the age of nineteen, the Nazis had robbed him of his youth. The son of a Jewish livestock dealer, Frankenthal had been forced at age fourteen to work in a Jewish labor brigade building and repairing roads until the Nazis deported his family and him to Auschwitz. He and his brother were "employed" as slave laborers to help build I. G. Farben's synthetic rubber and petroleum works at Monowitz, near the Auschwitz death camp. Toward the end of the war the two brothers were conscripted to work in one of the notorious underground rocket factories known collectively as the Mittelbau. The so-called tunnel factories were located near the town of Nordhausen in the midst of the Hartz Mountains, not far from Weimar, where the poet Goethe spent the greater part of his life. The Red Army liberated Hans and his brother in Theresienstadt.

After returning to his hometown, Frankenthal had to cope with the fact that it no longer had any Jewish residents. He was also forced to realize that no one was interested in hearing about his horrible experiences or the suffering endured by Jews in general during the Nazi period.

Only after Frankenthal retired did he find the strength to speak openly about his past. He became a member of the Central Council of Jews in Germany and a representative of the Association of Critical Shareholders of "I. G. Farben in Liquidation"—a firm more interested in recovering its assets in the former East Germany than in providing restitution to its former slave laborers. Up until his death in December 1999, Frankenthal tried to draw attention to the plight of these exploited unfortunates.

Hans Frankenthal was born in 1926 in the town of Schmallenberg in the Sauerland region of Germany. Together with his family he was deported to Auschwitz in 1943. He and his brother survived forced labor in the Monowitz and Mittelbau-Dora concentration camps. They were liberated in 1945 in Theresienstadt. After returning to Schmallenberg, the author ran a butcher shop and worked as a livestock dealer. He served on the Regional Association of the Jewish Communities of Westphalia and Lippe (Landesverband der jüdischen Gemeinden Westfalen-Lippe) and the Central Council of Jews in Germany. He was also deputy chairman of the Auschwitz Committee in the Federal Republic of Germany.

The Unwelcome One

Part I

"Where Is Schmallenberg?"

Our bus stopped at a hotel a few kilometers outside of Dresden. We got off—that is, the twenty people, all from the Dortmund area, who were to stay there overnight.

My brother Ernst and I shared a room. We crawled into the double bed with its thick mattresses and pulled the quilts up over ourselves. Our heads were nearly enveloped by the soft pillows. Half an hour later we were still tossing from one side to the other, from right to left and left to right.

"Hans," Ernst suddenly asked me in a low voice, "so you can't fall asleep either?"

"I don't understand. I'm tired but I can't close my eyes."

I kept on tossing beneath the covers until I finally made up my mind. "Ernst, in ten minutes I'm going to be sound asleep."

I lay down on the floor, grabbed my pillow, and quickly fell into a deep slumber.

Our bodies weren't used to lying on something soft or to being covered—we had spent the last two years in the camps.

Just a few days earlier, Ernst and I had given a brief account of the past few years to a commission in Theresienstadt. Afterward we were asked where we wished to be sent. "We'd like to go to Schmallenberg" was our reply.

"Where is Schmallenberg?"

When we answered that Schmallenberg was in Germany, the members of the commission stared at us in disbelief. "How can you go back to a country that has done such horrible things to you?"

I woke up long before sunrise, as I usually did, and thought hard about the question. We hoped to see our relatives and friends there again, but it was the final words spoken to us by our father as we were separated from one another that was the critical factor in our decision.

My brother and I were headed back to Schmallenberg in the Sauerland region of North Rhine–Westphalia, where we had spent our childhood.

The Boycott

As I was walking home from school one day—I was six years old at the time—I saw some SA men standing in front of the four Jewish businesses in Schmallenberg.[1] They were carrying signs that read: "Germans, defend yourselves—don't buy from Jews!" The Nazis had even posted Brownshirts in front of my Uncle Emil's butcher shop. Bewildered, I ran to tell my parents what I had seen. The date was 1 April 1933.

The mood at home wasn't exactly upbeat, but at the same time, my father didn't seem to be very worried. Together with three of his brothers he ran a livestock trading business, and, as he did every Saturday around five o'clock in the afternoon, he went that day to the stationmaster's office. There he arranged for the cattle he had bought during the week to be shipped to the livestock markets in Elberfeld and Dortmund.

I was sitting with my uncles and the other Jewish livestock dealers in our living room when my father returned in a depressed mood and told us that the boycott of Jewish businesses also applied to the shipping of livestock by rail.

This was, of course, a major blow to the livestock dealers. That afternoon Heinrich Reinke, a friend of my father's from the neighboring town of Oberkirchen and himself a livestock dealer, came up with a solution. Before going to the railroad station to arrange for the shipment of livestock, he warned the men that "we're going to have enormous problems tomorrow" and that "the only thing to do is to alter the records."

As expected, Hermann Gilsbach, the *Ortsgruppenleiter* (local group leader), accompanied by a police captain, appeared first at our house and then at Heinrich Reinke's. He demanded to see the records of the business and then proceeded to scrutinize them. The evening before, however, my father and Reinke had sat down after nightfall to change the entries in the account books. Heinrich Reinke had been made to appear as the sole buyer and seller. However, the Nazis still wanted to know: "How come you're shipping livestock for Jews?"

They could hardly wait to take legal action against Reinke. But my father's friend was a clever fellow and insisted, "This is the first real chance I've had to fleece the Jews. By buying the cattle at half price, I'm paying them back for all the times they cheated me."

The Nazis apparently bought his argument and the matter ended there.

Until that time, the Jewish livestock dealers in the region hadn't had any major difficulties. The first Jewish family to settle in Schmallenberg had arrived in the late seventeenth century. By the early 1930s there were eleven Jewish families—50 people in all—living in a town with a total population of 2,500. Most of the Jews were employed in the cattle trade or as butchers. One of the families, however, had played a critical role in building and consolidating the local textile industry, becoming well known and highly respected beyond Schmallenberg itself. The brothers Michael and Simon Stern owned a textile business that produced mainly hand-knitted articles. In 1867, however, they expanded their factory to include a wool-spinning mill. As a result the Stern family was considered a major contributor to the development of a modern textile industry in Schmallenberg. In time the Salomon Stern Knitwear Factory had sales offices in both Schmallenberg and the city of Wuppertal.

My family had lived in Schmallenberg for generations and was completely integrated into the social and economic life of the town. My grandfather, David Frankenthal, moved to Schmallenberg in 1880 from Altenlotheim in Hesse and married Emma Stern, whose family had been living in Schmallenberg for three generations. In 1890 he built a house with a butcher shop attached to it, which is where my father Max was born in 1883, as well as his sister Selma and his four brothers—Josef, Julius, Emil, and Sally.

Overcoming family opposition, Aunt Selma broke a taboo and married a Christian, Karl Friedrich. While Uncle Emil took charge of the butcher shop, his brothers were busy building the livestock trading business. My father was put in charge of the operation and made responsible for billing and keeping the books. The Frankenthal brothers traveled the length and breadth of the Sauerland on their buying trips and were well thought of.

In 1910 my father became the first Jew in Schmallenberg to win the title of champion marksman at the local rifle club. Since the middle of the nineteenth century the Jews of Schmallenberg had been trying to become members of the club, but it wasn't until the late 1860s that the Stern brothers succeeded in changing the club rules and gaining admittance. In subsequent decades a number of other clubs—with the exception of the Catholic Kolping Society—opened their doors to Jews. Social and recreational associations such as the rifle club, the men's chorus, the bowling club, and various sports enthusiasts' clubs played an important role in the lives of Schmallenberg's citizens; membership in them gave people a certain standing in society.

My father and his brothers were active-duty soldiers during the First World War. Like other patriotic Germans my father fought for "emperor, nation and fatherland." He was awarded the Iron Cross Second Class and was discharged as a sergeant. After the war he became a member of the veterans' association and was very involved in helping erect Schmallenberg's first war memorial.

Like most of the rural population he was a nationalist and politically conservative, and like the great majority of Schmallenberg's other residents he voted for the Catholic Center Party.

We children often heard him say, "I'm proud to be a German Jew."

My parents became acquainted in the early 1920s in Schmallenberg while my mother, Adele (born in 1886), was living with her mother in Duisburg. She was descended from a family of butchers in Krefeld. But after her father was killed in a slaughterhouse by a rampaging bull, her mother sold the butcher shop and opened a boardinghouse in Duisburg. My parents met while my mother was accompanying a girl-friend of hers, Helene Funke, on a visit to Helene's hometown. Helene had been born in Schmallenberg but had settled in Duisburg, where she ran a dressmaking shop. My father was nearly forty at the time and still unmarried. After the war he had decided to give priority to re-building his business. My parents were engaged in 1923 and married a year later. Their first son, my brother Ernst, was born on 18 July 1924. I was born two years later on 15 June 1926.

Our Jewish Home

My mother was a genteel woman with a solid middle-class upbring-ing. Although she didn't quite fit into a rural environment, she got on very well with the people of Schmallenberg. Unlike my aunts, though, she would never be seen in a cowshed, which was hardly surprising, given the fact that she wouldn't have known what to do there. She didn't have the slightest idea how to groom or milk a cow. On the other hand, she managed the family's finances, maintained a strictly Orthodox Jewish household, and acted as a calming influence in our lives. Being Orthodox, she made sure that we had a religious upbringing and observed the Jewish law. At home, for example, we kept kosher.

Holidays played a very important role in our family life, and our mother—who was an excellent cook—would serve a veritable feast on those special days. After consuming six or seven courses, my father would lean back in his chair with a slight groan and mumble his "Am I ever full." Then my mother would smile to herself and tease him, saying, "Well, I suppose you don't have any room for dessert then," after which he would offer his standard riposte—"You always have room for dessert, even when you're full." Naturally, we children mimicked him.

With only eleven Jewish families, it wasn't easy to provide a Jewish education for children in a town as small as Schmallenberg. A large majority of the population, like the children next door whom we grew up with, were Catholic. Protestants and Jews were in the minority. Our mother didn't want us to eat non-kosher food in our friends' homes. Otherwise, though, our Jewishness mattered little or not at all. We were allowed to go to the Christian cemetery with our gentile friends on All Saints' Day and visit them on Christmas Eve when they opened their presents. After all, we got presents, too—during Hanukkah.

My mother made one exception, however. She didn't want us to go to the Catholic kindergarten. She thought that the nuns would try to convert us.

My father was also Orthodox, but like most of the other Jews in Schmallenberg he tended to be liberal in matters of religion. Since most of the Jewish men worked in the livestock trade or in the slaughterhouse and conducted the major part of their business on Friday and Saturday, that is, the Shabbat, they couldn't observe all the religious laws. But as soon as he found time, our father would go with us to the synagogue in Schmallenberg, where we would take our place next to him, one son on his left side and one on his right. If we showed a lack of interest during the service or our eyes wandered instead of looking at the prayer book, he would admonish us by pointing to the passage being read by the rabbi or intoned by the cantor. The Jewish community in Schmallenberg was like one big family. The heads of the eleven families just managed to provide the minimum number of male adults needed for communal prayer. The prayers were read by Heinemann Funke, the designated leader of the community, or by the father of Julius Goldschmidt. During the High Holy Days and on other special occasions, a rabbi from Hesse would be invited to conduct services.

During many of the holidays, Ernst and I had to stay in the synagogue for as much as five hours—and on Yom Kippur for twelve to thirteen hours. This was particularly vexing when friends on the outside would call me to come out and play with them. My father, though, insisted that we remain seated. He succeeded in raising us to be devout Jews. And—following his example—I grew up proud to be a Jew.

Community life played an important role in Jewish families. In other respects, however, there was little to distinguish Jews from the rest of the town's population. In no sense did the Jews live in isolation; my father had many non-Jewish friends and acquaintances. He went to play cards three times a week, each night in a different tavern. He kept one of his long pipes in each of the taverns he frequented, so that all he needed to take with him from home was his tobacco pouch and some matches. He would get together with, among others, Franz Falke, the head of the Falke Company, a farmer named Kewekordes, and Hepelmann, the building contractor who built our house on Obringhauserstraße in 1926–27. They would play skat or whist or a German card game called *Doppelkopf*.

I still remember how he would occasionally let me accompany him on his daily visit to the barbershop. Customers who regularly had a shave there had their own porcelain shaving mugs hung in a long row inside the shop; my father's bore the number 14.

My Childhood in Schmallenberg

In 1932 I began attending the Catholic elementary school in Schmallenberg. The Jewish children got along quite well with the Catholic youngsters, whose parents had told them, "You can play with the Jews but not with the Lutherans!" I couldn't understand why the Protestant children were isolated from the rest of us and had to attend a school in the neighboring town. One of my best playmates, Erwin Wolf, who lived four houses down from us, came from a Protestant family. There were three Jewish children in my class. Besides me there was Else, the daughter of Uncle Julius, and Edith Gonsenhäuser. During my days at school it was customary for Catholic children to attend Mass before formal instruction began. In addition, the first hour of class was devoted to religious instruction. So the Jewish pupils didn't have to start their school day until 8:30 A.M. Naturally, this gave rise to a lot of envy among our classmates. On the other hand, we didn't really have such a big advantage, because our religious instruction took place on Sunday, when we were given private lessons between one and five in the afternoon from Albert Stern, a teacher from Berleburg. Then it was our classmates who would romp outside and call to us from beneath the window: "Come on out—let's play soccer!"

The fact that my uncle had only daughters had a great impact on my childhood. As the only male progeny in the family, Ernst and I were spoiled by our aunts and uncles as well as by our parents. I was so wild about the animals and the stables that my mother had trouble getting me to do my homework. As soon as I finished my school assignments, I would dash off to help clean the dung out of the cowshed or milk the cows. So I ended up spending a large part of my childhood with my uncles and aunts. Ernst, on the other hand, wasn't particularly interested in the livestock business. Unlike me, he enjoyed staying at home and helping my mother in the kitchen. In fact, for some time he even considered becoming a ship's cook. That was probably one of the reasons my relatives focused their attention on me. Sometimes they would kid me and tell me to grow faster so that I could get a driver's license that much sooner. There was a plan to buy some motorized transportation for the business. But since my father felt he was too old to learn how to drive, he chose to take the early morning train twice a week to the Henneborn district. There he would order a taxi to pick him up and drive him to the edge of the various towns and villages he planned to visit. He would then walk from house to house to conduct his business.

During school vacations he allowed me to accompany him on his business trips, as did my uncles. They would actually quarrel occasionally over who would get to take me with them the next day. This was all very exciting for me, especially since it was my job to buy the goatskins collected by my father's friend Wilhelm Piskuping—for what seemed like the princely sum of 25 pfennigs apiece. I dried them and stored them in our warehouse until Kasrael, a Jew from Hallenberg who dealt in hides and stopped by our place every two to three weeks, bought them from me. Since I was made responsible for this part of the business, I was permitted to keep the proceeds and deposit them in a savings account.

Once during a summer vacation while my father and I were making our customary circuit of the villages, we got very hungry. Normally Father would ask a farmer for a slice of bread and five eggs, that is, a kosher meal. This time, however, he asked me if I felt like having a ham sandwich. "Just don't tell your mother!" he warned me.

When we got home I hopped into the bathtub first. Since I often smelled of the cowshed, this was hardly unusual. While my mother was scrubbing my back, she began questioning me. "Well, how did it go? Did you have anything to eat?"

"Yes, I did."

"Well, what did you have?"

"A ham sandwich and eggs."

She dropped the sponge and glowered. I thought she was going to throttle me. I had never seen my parents fight before, but that day I heard loud voices coming from downstairs in the living room and words being exchanged.

I was pretty unruly as a boy and caused my parents quite a bit of trouble. When I was seven or eight my friends and I made a slingshot. With our little catapult in hand, we headed for the tar-paper factory that was located about two hundred meters from our house. Karl Pieper, a friend of my father's, was the owner. The factory was housed in a long building that had hundreds of tiny windows—in other words, the perfect target! We proceeded to break one window after another. . . .

The row that followed was nothing to sneeze at!

We played a lot of pranks. For instance, we tied a string around a wallet, hid it in a ditch, and pulled it away whenever someone bent over to pick it up. Or we took the adhesive off beer bottles and used it to stick flathead screws onto windows to scare old people. At school, on the other hand, I was well behaved and diligent. My mother saw to that.

The Sports Festival

After the 1933 boycott the livestock business dropped off precipitously, despite the fact that a number of people were still undeterred by the appeals to anti-Semitism and continued to patronize Jewish businesses. Every town had its *Ortsgruppenleiter* and its *Ortsbauernführer* (local farmers' leader). Consequently the farmers who still had dealings with us were made to pay a price for their loyalty. They were discriminated against, for instance, when special allotments of seed were distributed.

Nevertheless, the regional Nazi Party propagandists felt they had to keep hammering away at what they regarded as an unsatisfactory state of affairs. For example, an article appeared in their newspaper *Rote Erde* (*Red Earth*) titled "Stay Away from Jews! People Still Aren't Getting the Message," in which the author threatened to publish the names of those who continued to maintain a business relationship with Jews, reviling them as "Jew lackeys" and "traitors to the nation and the state."

From 1935, Jews conducted their livestock business secretly—mainly at night. The few farmers who still sold us cattle were afraid to bring them to us personally. Fortunately, though, there were people in Schmallenberg who would pick them up for us for a fee. If they happened to be unavailable, my father would put a rope in my hand in the dark of night and say: "Here's the money—now go pick up the cow."

On one occasion I tried to wriggle out of the job, telling my father, "It's dark—I can't see a thing."

"Then feel your way there."

On another occasion I tried to get out of picking up a cow from a farmer named Huckel who lived in Berghausen. "But I don't have any idea where Huckel lives."

"Then ask."

The increasing discrimination against Jews was a constant subject of discussion at home. Uncle Ernst, my mother's brother, wanted to send us out of the room when talk turned to political matters, but my father objected: "This concerns the boys as much as it does us. They might as well listen."

Personally, I didn't find the atmosphere in Schmallenberg particularly oppressive. My early years at school were nothing out of the ordinary, even though there were fervent anti-Semites and SA men on the teaching staff. There was Rüther, the physical education instructor, for example, who made everybody assemble in the schoolyard to sing *Deutschland über alles* and the Horst Wessel Song.[2] The Jewish students were dismissed and sent home before such events took place.

Relations between Jewish and non-Jewish children were quite good until 1935—the year the Nuremberg Laws were passed. That was the year problems began to emerge for me. Like most of my friends I was an ardent sports enthusiast. We did gymnastics as members of the Deutscher Turnerbund (German Gymnastics Federation) and played soccer in the Deutsche Jugendkraft, the Catholic sports association; we bicycled in the summer and skied in the nearby mountains in the winter. The annual school sports festival was a major event for us. During the 1935 festival, however, a voice suddenly came across the square while the competitions were still in progress: "Jew children report to the festival director!"

From the language used, we knew something was wrong; until then we been called "Jewish" children in Schmallenberg—never "Jew" children. Not knowing what to expect, we went to see the festival director, who told us: "Jews have no business being at a German sports festival."

The teachers took away the oak leaf wreaths we had made before the festival and the awards we had received. Despondent, Ernst and I sneaked home and told our father what had happened. We urged him to leave the country, but he reassured us: "Nothing can happen to us. I fought for the fatherland."

Like many of his acquaintances who had taken part in the First World War, he assumed that anti-Semitism was directed mainly against East European Jews, most of whom lived in the Scheunenviertel section of Berlin.

That same week, Ernst and I went to the public swimming pool, where a sign had recently been posted at the entrance: "No entry to Jews!" Since the pool attendant was a family friend, we were still able to get in. But just a few days later he informed us that he could no longer allow us to enter.

Our father's attempt during the following months to found a Jewish sports club fell through because the Jewish communities in the Sauerland simply didn't have enough people.

All at once, engaging in competitive sports became a thing of the past.

Losing My Friends

It was during these months that I lost most of my friends. The Deutscher Turnerbund and the Deutsche Jugendkraft were incorporated into the Hitler Youth, and everybody in my class was made a member of the Jungvolk. One day my classmates were taken to a fabric shop and issued Nazi uniforms, except for two boys whose parents refused to have their sons wear the new outfits. These boys continued to stand by us, but we were more or less shunned by the other children. Consequently we needed a lot of moral support from our parents.

In the winter I visited my uncles and aunts. They owned some pastureland that was perfect for sledding. Other children couldn't chase us away from there. But the days when someone would hop onto our sled with us or when we used to tie three or four sleds together were gone forever.

When I asked some of my former friends why they were avoiding us, they invited me to drop by one of their classes and listen to the things the teacher was saying about all the bad Jews. What I discovered they were learning was that we Jews were lower on the scale of evolution than rats—and that's exactly how our "Aryan" classmates began to treat us.

Things at school went from bad to worse. Instead of reciting morning prayers, the boys and girls repeated Hitler Youth slogans. Crucifixes disappeared from the walls, only to be replaced by pictures of Hitler—which were hung on the very same nails. And when students sang the Horst Wessel Song and the first stanza of the national anthem on Nazi holidays, we were ordered to leave the classroom.

My homeroom teacher, Fräulein Kohlpott, was friendly to us; during her class I sat near the front of the room in the second row of desks. Of the other ten or twelve teachers, though, half were ardent Nazis.

Messner and Rüther, for instance, came to school in their SA uniforms. When I was in their class, they would order me to sit in the back of the room. The next morning, however, when I was about to take my seat in the last row again, Fräulein Kohlpott would say: "Come up here and sit in the front." Rüther, my physical education teacher, once saw me sparring with a classmate during recess and remarked mockingly: "Look, Jews can box." The Nazis depicted Jews as base cowards. "A craven Jew boxing a German boy. Say, let's have our next P. E. class over in the indoor shooting range where we can do a little boxing."

An hour later Rüther took us to the huge gymnasium that housed the shooting range. In the middle of the building, where the band usually played, there was a kind of boxing ring. Rüther took out the boxing gloves he had brought with him and ordered me to fight the other students. A real boxing match ensued: rounds of two minutes' duration and one minute between rounds. He kept sending bigger and seemingly stronger opponents into the ring, but none of them could knock me down. I felt quite satisfied with myself.

Rüther got very upset and insulted the other boys: "You mean you can't even get the better of a cowardly Jew? What a disgrace you all are!"

After school I returned home in triumph and told my parents how successful I had been. At first my father beamed, but then he turned to me and asked: "Do you think you did the right thing?"

"Yes," I declared, "and I'm going to keep on defending myself."

A short time later one of my classmates started calling me names as I was walking home from school—"Kike with a nose like a spike." In a flash I dropped my knapsack and pounced on him.

No sooner did I arrive home than my father, who had seen the two of us while he was standing on our property, asked me what had happened.

"He insulted me and called us names . . . so I beat him up."

My father reprimanded me: "Let that be the last time." He told me never again to do such a thing and explained that we Jews had been deprived of our rights. However, "We are proud of the fact that we are Jews—even if we have no rights!"

There were only a few people in Schmallenberg who in spite of everything refused to be intimidated and stood by us. Daniel Marburger, a building contractor, helped my father in the dead of night to connect our main line to the newly built Reichsbahn (German railway) sewerage system. Prior to that time we had had a three-compartment septic tank. As Marburger and my father were installing the line, however, Ferdinand Hütemann, a municipal employee and Nazi Party member, observed the two of them and reported their activities to the local authorities. As a result, they were ordered to dig up the line; however, Marburger was such a skilled craftsman that he nevertheless managed to maintain a functioning connection to the Reichsbahn's waste disposal system. Since Marburger wasn't an anti-Semite, he was written up in the Jew-baiting newspaper *Der Stürmer* and denounced as a "Jew lover."

The First Arrests

In 1937 my father was arrested during Yom Kippur services and taken away from the synagogue by the police. He returned a few hours later and told us that Christian livestock dealers had filed charges against him. They accused him of having tampered with the livestock scale in Fredeburg and of having swindled farmers. However, testimony by the owner of the scale, who was also the weigher, led to prompt dismissal of the charges. The weigher testified under oath that my father had never laid hands on the scale and that no animal had been put on the scale that he, the owner of the scale, hadn't weighed himself.

Julius Goldschmidt was also arrested that same year. He owned a butcher shop and made his customary circuit of the surrounding villages every weekend to deliver his wares. In the village of Rehsiepen, twenty kilometers from Schmallenberg, a sixteen- or seventeen-year-old girl had asked if she could ride back with him. She said that she wanted to buy some shoes.

Goldschmidt drove with the girl to Schmallenberg. She subsequently went to Tillmann's shoe store. Frau Falke-Tillmann, the sister of Ortsgruppenleiter Gilsbach, became curious and asked her: "How did you get to Schmallenberg at this time of day?"

"I drove with Herr Goldschmidt."

"Did Herr Goldschmidt do anything to you?"

"No—nothing."

Frau Falke-Tillmann nevertheless continued to probe: "You mean he didn't touch you?"

"Well, yes, he patted me on the shoulder or whatever."

The Ortsgruppenleiter's sister promptly informed the police that Goldschmidt was guilty of *Rassenschande,* that is, of defiling the "Aryan" race. Since Goldschmidt was the kind of person who by nature didn't let people walk all over him, the local Nazis probably had it in for him anyway. Earlier he had poked fun at a Schmallenberg Brownshirt by the name of Seppels Emil—a runt of a man invariably short of money and always dressed in his storm trooper uniform. In the Wüllner beer hall Goldschmidt had publicly offered to give the SA man 10 marks: "Here are ten marks—now go get drunk!" Seppels Emil, in full dress uniform, took the money. He was subsequently summoned to appear before the local party leaders, who hauled him over the coals.

The events surrounding Goldschmidt's arrest left a deep impression on me. A throng marched down our street at night and started singing "When Jew blood flies from our knives, things will be fine again."

Before Goldschmidt was arrested the crowd proceeded to wreck his butcher shop and ransack his apartment. He was sentenced to six months in prison for defiling the "Aryan" race. After serving his sentence he was sent directly to Sachsenhausen concentration camp.

The process of "Aryanization" (*Arisierung*) began in 1937. A number of Jews in Schmallenberg were forced to close their businesses because of a decline in sales. My father, though, refused to give up his business, in spite of the fact that things were going from bad to worse.

The end finally came in October 1938, when the authorities forcibly shut down the Jewish livestock dealers' businesses in the Sauerland by withdrawing their peddler's licenses. Although some Jews continued to sell individual animals, arguing that selling them was simply part of the business of operating a farm, they ran the growing risk of being informed on. Whenever a Jew was spotted taking a cow through town, the authorities checked the next day to determine whether the animal was being sold as part of a commercial enterprise or merely for agricultural purposes. Most of the informers were "Aryan" livestock dealers taking advantage of their privileged position.

Soon afterward the first livestock cooperatives were established. Farmers had to hand over their livestock to the cooperative and lost direct control over the sale of their goods. They had no idea where their cattle were being put up for sale, and they didn't receive compensation for at least a week. When the farmers had sold their cows to us, they would deliver them promptly at a mutually agreeable time and were immediately paid in cash.

It came as a hard blow to my father when after October 1938 he was no longer permitted to make his customary rounds of the towns and villages. Most peddler's licenses, however, permitted the licensees to deal in hides as well as engage in the livestock trade. So the Frankenthals kept themselves afloat by buying up hides from farmers who did their own slaughtering.

The Pogrom

On 10 November 1938 I went to school as usual. I had celebrated my twelfth birthday in the summer and was in my sixth year of school. Just before noon recess about ten uniformed SA men burst into our classroom and shouted at the teacher, "Are there any Jew children in your school?"

"Of course we have Jewish children here," Bergental, the principal and my homeroom teacher, replied calmly but firmly. He was a devout Catholic but not an anti-Semite. When the SA men barked, "All the Jew children are under arrest," Bergental rang the recess bell. He told me later that he had hoped the Brownshirts wouldn't be able to nab anyone while all the children were running out of the classroom at the same time. But the Nazis had cordoned off the school entrance, and the storm troopers took eleven Jewish children between the ages of six and thirteen into custody.

They then took us to the courthouse, where I ran into my father, who had been arrested along with other Jewish men in town. When I asked him what was going on, all he said was, "They set fire to the synagogue and wrecked our house." Later we learned that the SA had smashed the window of Uncle Emil's butcher shop with an ax, taken the meat that was on display, and thrown it into the street. They had also plundered Uncle Sally's home, beating and severely injuring him. And in Duisburg that night, storm troopers ransacked Uncle Ernst's apartment, slitting open his down-filled bedcovers and tossing his piano out the window. The Nazis euphemistically referred to the pogrom as *Kristallnacht* ("Crystal Night" or "Night of Broken Glass").

In the course of the day, the other Jews were brought to the courthouse as well, with one exception—Artur Stern. Later he told us that he had heard about the pogrom in Elberfeld, went to the railroad station, boarded a train, and traveled all over Germany for two days—and so escaped the Nazis.

At the approach of evening the women and children were released and sent home, while the men were confined to a homeless shelter.

That night we were allowed to bring them food. The next morning, however, my mother returned home in a state of total confusion. None of the men were in the courthouse.

Later that day Police Captain Krawitz appeared at our home and informed us that he had transferred the men to the Steinwache in Dortmund, a Gestapo prison. Then he gave my mother a short note from my father: "We're being taken away—don't do anything until you hear from me."

A few days later Amtsinspektor Holthaus appeared at our door and ordered my mother to ask all the Jewish women to come to her home that evening.[3]

It was already dark by the time Ortsgruppenleiter Gilsbach, Mayor Riese, Amtsinspektor Holthaus, and a senior SA official named Tigges appeared before the women who had gathered in my mother's living room. Sitting in the corner, I was able to observe Holthaus. He did all the talking.

"We've prepared papers to document that you've sold your entire assets to deserving members of the Party."

Holthaus hadn't finished speaking when my mother broke in. "I—I mean none of us is going to sign anything without talking to our husbands first!"

Holthaus looked her up and down coldly: "If you don't sign this evening, you're never going to see your husbands alive again. They've already been transferred from Dortmund to the Sachsenhausen concentration camp near Berlin."

He went on to say that the men could be released from the camp after the sales had been confirmed, but that the women had to sign first. This was, of course, nothing less than outright blackmail.

Before the uninvited guests left, they revealed the names of the

"Aryan" buyers. The homes and assets of Schmallenberg's Jews were divided up among the town's most zealous Nazis. Those who had extorted the signatures were the first to help themselves: the town council seized my father's property; Amtsinspektor Holthaus "acquired" Uncle Sally's and Uncle Julius's house, together with Uncle Emil's butcher shop.

When we were alone again I asked my mother, "Why did you sign, when Father explicitly told you not to do anything without him?"

"What's property or a house compared to a human life?"

"I Would Never Have Believed What the Germans Are Capable Of"

The non-Jews in town resigned themselves to the fact of the pogrom and didn't protest—with one exception: Dina Falke, the mother of the manufacturer Franz Falke. She stood on the street and started ranting about what people had done to the Jews. Her family, however, quickly saw to it that she was taken home. Most of the other citizens of Schmallenberg adopted a wait-and-see attitude or welcomed and supported the riots. It was said, for example, that the livestock dealer Robert Krämer supplied the straw that was used to set fire to the synagogue. This was a plausible allegation, since he benefited greatly from the fact that the Jewish livestock dealers had been driven out of business. As early as 1937 he had been observed at night going from his farm to Max Stern's shop and breaking the windows with a stick.

Because of his youth—he was only fourteen—my brother Ernst was released after just a few days in prison; the adult men returned home late at night on 28 November.

My father was a broken man. His head shaved and his clothing completely crumpled, he sat at the table ignoring the questions we kept heaping on him. Where had he been? What had they done to him? All he said now and then was: "Let's get out of this place!" and "I'm not allowed to say anything, and I'm not going to say anything."

I kept pumping him for information but always received the same answer. Hearing that my father had returned to town, Daniel Marburger sneaked into our house through the back door that same night and asked him similar questions: "Where were you? What did they do to all of you?"

Marburger kept pressing until my father was at his wits' end and replied, "I would never have believed what the Germans are capable of." That was all anyone could get out of him.

The next day the released Kristallnacht prisoners had to report to Amtsinspektor Holthaus to sign a document stating that they agreed to the "sale" of their property. For our residence, with its stables and yard, the five or so acres of pastureland that produced the hay and feed for our livestock, and our other property, our family was paid the ridiculous sum of 13,000 reichsmarks (RM). Five thousand RM of this amount was deposited in a blocked account administered by the Gestapo from which my father was allowed to withdraw 250 RM a month. The remaining 8,000 RM was sent to the internal revenue authorities in Münster. The Jewish community was not only made liable for the damage to property resulting from the pogrom, it also had to pay a "fine" of 1 billion reichsmarks.

My father wondered how the Jews could ever come up with that much money. But a short time later it became evident how much of the fine was covered by the property the Nazis had stolen through the process of "Aryanization."

The former Kristallnacht prisoners had to pledge to leave Germany within a few weeks together with their families or at least to prove that they had made an effort to do so. Otherwise they would be taken into custody again and sent to a concentration camp.

My parents tried everything they could think of to get out of Germany. Their plan to send Ernst and me to England with one of the Kindertransports fell through. I still remember the big black suitcases with our names written on them. Friends of my father, however, questioned the idea of sending unaccompanied children so far away from home. They tried to reassure him that National Socialism was a passing phenomenon, that Hitler would start a war and that everything would be over in six months. I no longer recall the exact reason, but Ernst and I never did get on a Kindertransport train and find shelter in Great Britain.[4]

Finally, in the summer of 1939, a second cousin in America guaranteed the 250 dollars per person required to meet the criteria for affidavits of financial support that prospective immigrants needed in order to enter the United States. Hitler's attack on Poland, however, and the subsequent beginning of the war made escape impossible. A few other things would happen, though, before we reached that point. The Nazis enacted one anti-Jewish measure after another. All Jewish men had to add *Israel* to their name, and all Jewish women, *Sara.* We were only permitted to go shopping for two hours a day, and after 8:00 P.M. we were forbidden to leave our residences or even to step out on our balconies. At some point we began to ask ourselves if we were permitted to do anything. From day to day, life became more and more difficult.

Starting in 1939, Jews weren't allowed to choose the kind of work they wished to do. The town put all Jews over the age of sixteen on forced labor. As part of the Nazis' so-called Labor Deployment *(Arbeitseinsatz),* the Jews in Schmallenberg were compelled to slave away in the woods and quarries or dig ponds to provide water to extinguish the fires that the Nazis expected as a result of the war they were planning. My father worked in the tar-paper factory owned by his friend Karl Pieper until Pieper was forbidden to employ Jews. He was then conscripted to work on forced-labor projects for the town and felt humiliated. His brother Emil had a stroke and died as a result of this backbreaking work.

It wasn't just the town, though, that exploited the Jews' labor. Individuals did so as well. Josef Gilsbach, the sluggardly Ortsbauernführer and brother of Ortsgruppenleiter Hermann Gilsbach, for example, had neglected to weed his farm of beetroots before the onset of winter. So he turned to the town council and requested a contingent of forced laborers. The council duly provided him with a Jewish *Arbeitskolonne.*[5]

My mother suffered terribly under these conditions. She tried to commit suicide several times. Ernst, who was closer to her than I, often followed her to the storeroom and managed just in the nick of time to stop her from taking her life. I frequently observed the two of them discussing the mounting persecution, but I was probably too young at the time to comprehend the extent of the threat.

My Bar Mitzvah

My bar mitzvah took place in June 1939. The ceremony generally occurs on the Sabbath following a boy's thirteenth birthday and commemorates his religious adulthood within the Jewish community. Customarily seven men are called to read an assigned portion from the scroll of the Torah. When the bar mitzvah takes place, the young man is called up during the religious service to chant the conclusion of the portion of the day. He then has to recite prayers over a light celebratory repast following the service. The prayers last about ten minutes— even longer if the boy pronounces Hebrew clearly and correctly.

In 1938, before Kristallnacht, I spent four weeks during my school vacation traveling to the home of a teacher named Stern in the town of Berleburg. He gave me private lessons to prepare me for this important event.

As the time for my bar mitzvah approached, I conferred with my father about the fact that there weren't any more Torah scrolls in Schmallenberg for me to read from. The SA had stolen them from the synagogue together with other objects of value before they burned the building to the ground. My father recalled that Uncle Aaron, a butcher in Altenhundem, had rescued a Torah scroll and was keeping it in a safe place in his house. He suggested I go to see him and ask whether he would lend it to me.

That weekend I hopped on my bicycle and rode approximately eighteen kilometers to Uncle Aaron's.

After I explained my problem to him, he shook his head to express his regret. He did have a Torah scroll he would give me, he said, but it was *posel*, that is, the handwritten letters could no longer be easily read.[6] Sometimes Torah scribes are able to write over the illegible portions; however, if the ink has become brittle—because the scroll had been stored in a damp place, for instance—the scroll is declared unusable. And according to the Jewish law, like any object on which the name of God is written it has to be buried in the same way a person is laid to rest.

My dilemma seemed insoluble—I still needed an intact Torah scroll for my bar mitzvah—but after puzzling over the problem for a few minutes, I made a decision: "Better a scroll that's *posel* than no scroll at all. There's so much that's *posel* in Germany, it really doesn't matter anymore."

With an air of deliberation but a smile on his face, he nodded and carefully wrapped up the Torah scroll that I then carried with me as I bicycled back to Schmallenberg.

I could barely wait for 15 June, my birthday, and for the following Sabbath. After the synagogue was destroyed in the pogrom, we had set up a makeshift house of prayer in our house on Obringhauserstraße. That is where we celebrated my bar mitzvah, together with a close circle of friends and relatives who hadn't yet emigrated. It was a wonderful day for me, but when I think back to that time I realize how terrible the day must have been for my parents, who remembered similar events celebrated in freedom.

The "Jews' Houses"

In the summer of 1939 the town gave our house to an "Aryan" German, and like the ten other Jewish families in Schmallenberg we had to vacate it at very short notice and move into one of the so-called "Jews' houses." The front doors of these buildings were marked with a Star of David and were to remain unlocked at night. A list containing the names of all the residents had to be posted in every hallway so that any policeman on the beat could come in at any time during the day or night and take a head count of the occupants.

We were assigned three rooms and a kitchen. Still, the move was very hard on my mother. She often suffered from headaches. In the beginning she was secretly treated by our family physician, Dr. van Ackern. But the headaches became almost unbearable and my mother was having problems with her vision as well, so the doctor sent her to the only hospital in Cologne that still admitted Jews. My father and I accompanied her when she went for tests. She was given radiation treatment. And I remember noticing that she was losing more and more of the hair on the left side of her head. But nobody discussed the results of the tests with us children.

After Kristallnacht, Jewish children were forbidden to attend the Catholic school. So an alternative educational system was set up. Starting in the summer our class—the eleven girls and boys taught by Stern, our religion instructor—met in the "Jews' houses." Stern brought another student along with him from Berleburg, a boy by the name of Goldschmidt. Rolf Goldschmidt was an illegitimate child of an "Aryan" father and a Jewish mother, so according to the Nuremberg Laws he was considered a "half Jew." His father could have protected him, but he didn't want to admit that Rolf was his son. Rolf's mother and grandparents were too proud to insist publicly that he do so.

In the summer of 1940 the Dortmund office of the Gestapo closed down our little experiment in education and sent the students who were still of school age to various Jewish schools in Dortmund and Münster. For children aged seven to thirteen who were separated from their families and suddenly had to live with strangers, it was a depressing situation.

I had just turned fourteen and had completed my compulsory education, when my father decided to send me to one of the three vocational education programs that had been set up in 1937 by the Jewish community in Dortmund, where boys were trained to become locksmiths and cabinetmakers and girls to become seamstresses. As luck would have it, I ran into my brother, who had been taking a course for half a year to prepare himself for an apprenticeship as a locksmith. Being with him helped ease the trauma of separation from my parents.

The programs were set up to educate young Jews to become Zionists and prepare them for emigration to Palestine. So in addition to vocational training, we were taught about the Land of Israel and received instruction in English and *ivrit* and other subjects that would facilitate our emigration.[7]

"*Wheels Have to Roll to Win the War. . . .*"

In May 1941 the president of the Jewish community informed us that the Dortmund Gestapo had closed the vocational training school. We were told to report to the employment offices in our hometowns. Since Jews were normally forbidden to use public transportation, the Gestapo gave us a special pass so that Ernst and I could get back to Schmallenberg.

We reported to the employment office as ordered and were told to show up for work at the Lahrmann Road Construction Company in Meschede.

The company was brand new; it had not been in existence for more than six months. The director, Ferdinand Lahrmann, had worked in Arolsen for the regional studies association, and then for himself. He used his connections to secure construction contracts in the Waldeck region.

Lahrmann received us personally and then drove us to a construction site in Höringhausen, ten kilometers from Korbach.

There we were reunited with our father and worked together in the same labor brigade. We seldom saw our mother after we began working for Lahrmann, even though we were very concerned about leaving her alone. Special ordinances, however, prohibited Jews from going home if they worked more than seven kilometers from their hometown. They were to be separated from "Aryans" and housed in special quarters. Our work crew consisted of thirteen Jewish men from Schmallenberg and Brilon. We were packed into two trailers in which the Lahrmann Company had installed bunk beds. It was impossible for us to sit or stand together at one time.

In the summer the humid air nearly suffocated us, and in the winter we almost froze to death, since the walls consisted of nothing more than thin boards. We tried to heat the trailers by putting coal briquettes into a little stove, but when we got the fire going, moisture would build up on the interior walls. We had to stick wrapping paper on the ceiling so that the condensation wouldn't drip onto our heads. Later at night, after the stove went out, it got so cold that our blankets froze to the walls.

Even though building roads is backbreaking work for grown men, the regulations set down in the Youth Protection Act were suspended in our case. We were subject to the same working conditions as adults. I was barely fifteen years old and was forced to labor twelve to fourteen hours a day using a hand-operated tar sprayer. Beerhorst, the master butcher, and my brother spread the grit. Then while Max and Emil Stern, my father's cousins, pumped, I sprayed the tar. The rest of the *Arbeitskolonne* brought up the paving material.

Beerhorst supervised the work. Whenever Gestapo agents came to check on us, he always managed to have an amiable chat with them. Needless to say, he wasn't particularly friendly toward us. In fact, he invariably arranged the work in such a way that the boiling hot vapors from the tar blew directly into our faces. To protect our skin from being scalded, we mixed earth and water together to make a kind of clay that we rubbed on our faces.

Beginning in September 1941 we were required to wear a yellow badge on our clothing in the form of a six-pointed star; it had to be visible at all times. We were forbidden to appear in public without this distinguishing sign. Naturally, this applied to the construction site as well. I often wiped my tar-covered hands on the yellow star, but it didn't really help. Everyone knew we were part of a Jewish work gang.

During the hot summer months of 1942 the work was particularly hard. We began at 7:00 A.M., constantly exposed to the hot tar, with the sun beating down on our heads. By the afternoon I would be completely exhausted. One day I dropped the tar sprayer, dragged myself to a ditch, collapsed on the grass, and let out a moan. "I've had it. I can't stand it anymore. I want out."

Then as luck would have it, at that very moment Ferdinand Lahrmann showed up. Infuriated, he shouted at Beerhorst, "What's wrong with that guy over there?"

"The heat got to him. Says he can't go on."

Lahrmann's verbatim reply: "Turn the son of a gun over and let him have it!"

Maybe that is how people talk on construction sites, but it sounded pretty ominous to us.

Besides the brutal working conditions and the horrific accommodations, there was another problem: the provision of food supplies. The food rations we had been receiving since 1939 on the basis of our ration cards were far short of what we needed. The ration cards were stamped with a "J" for "Jew" and weren't valid for the purchase of milk, butter, peas and beans, or meat. The rations we received were just enough to keep us alive. Jews who were put on forced labor suffered from hunger if they couldn't somehow procure additional food. Many of them were completely emaciated and physically exhausted.

My father went to see Dr. van Ackern to help him obtain more food both for us and the other Schmallenberg Jews employed by Lahrmann. As an anti-Nazi, van Ackern had no qualms about providing a statement certifying my father's inability to return to work. The authorized sick leave gave my father time to travel to his former customers to barter the few valuables we had managed to keep after Kristallnacht and to go begging.

Besides the food my father got hold of for us in this way, there were some people in Schmallenberg who helped us without any urging. The woman who owned the König Café had a grocery attached to her establishment and was very kind to us. Her place of business was situated nearly opposite a "Jews' house," and whenever Frau König went to the Catholic boarding school run by nuns in our neighborhood, she would knock on my mother's window. No sooner did my mother open it than some food would sail through.

We still had to figure out how to smuggle food onto the construction site. Saturday was a regular working day and Sundays we usually had to unload the railway cars that brought in the material from the quarries in the Sauerland. On many of the cars someone had daubed the following slogan in white paint: "Wheels have to roll to win the war!" Whenever we saw it, we muttered to ourselves: "Nazi heads will have to roll after the war!" Since we weren't given any leave, we couldn't get off the construction site to pick up the food in Schmallenberg.

It was some time before we found out that the trackmaster was a reasonable person. He would secretly let us know on which Sundays no railway cars would be arriving. Ernst and I would then hop on our bicycles—in spite of the prohibition, we had nonetheless managed to obtain a couple—and ride to Schmallenberg by way of Höringhausen, Korbach, Medebach, and Winterberg. We would pick up the food and often ride back the same night so that we would be sure to show up for work on time on Monday. Thanks to this fortunate set of circumstances, we were more or less well nourished and fit. We had no idea that this would help save our lives in the months to come.

One day something very unusual happened. While we were working at the site, a butcher rode by in a horse-drawn carriage loaded with a couple of pigs. He addressed us in flawless Lauschen-Kaudesch, the argot of the Jewish livestock dealers that is related to Yiddish and was often spoken at the cattle markets.[8] After a brief conversation, the butcher—whose name was Sauer—invited us to visit him in the village that evening.

At dusk Ernst and I sneaked away. When we arrived at Sauer's place, he gave us a package of sausage, meat, and other food that he had specially wrapped for us. He even asked whether we had enough bread. When we told him we didn't, he walked us two houses down to the home of the master baker. Loaded down with sausage, meat, and bread, we headed back to the construction site. Needless to say, we were immensely grateful for this unusual gesture of support.

After Dr. van Ackern had written two or three medical reports exempting my father from work, he said that the Gestapo was giving him trouble and that he could no longer treat my father. When my father asked van Ackern whom he should turn to for medical care, van Ackern suggested Dr. Schwarze. My father must have been thunderstruck, because Schwarze was a leader in the Hitler Youth and regularly appeared before his patients in a Nazi uniform, resplendent with medals.

When my father finally summoned the courage to see Dr. Schwarze, it turned out that he wasn't really such an ardent Nazi after all, and like Dr. van Ackern he provided my father with statements excusing him from work. In time my father even managed to get Dr. Schwarze to issue him a certificate of disability. This allowed him not only to help supply us with food but to have additional time to look after our mother, whose condition was becoming progressively worse. On the other hand, of course, having a certificate of disability was potentially quite risky, for in early 1942 the first contingent of Jews in our region was already being "resettled" elsewhere. The story was that they were being sent to Poland; however, it didn't take much imagination to figure out that this wasn't the whole truth, because those who were sent on the transports were never heard from again—there were no letters, no postcards, nothing.

The Gestapo ordered the Jewish community in Dortmund to appoint some of its members to take their fellow Jews to the assembly areas. My father was one of the people charged with this sad task. He was responsible for making sure the Jewish men and women of Schmallenberg showed up as scheduled at the assembly areas in Dortmund. He was even forced to accompany his own relatives there and watch as they boarded the trains. He told us very little about what he had observed, however. Only once, during the second deportation, after he had sent off his Aunt Anna Stern, who was over eighty—a very old and frail woman—did Father make a remark: "Hopefully, she'll die soon." Although he obviously had some foreboding, he still hoped that able-bodied Jews would not be deported.

In Broad Daylight

On 26 February 1943, Lahrmann suddenly turned up at the construction site. "All of you," he announced, "have been ordered to appear tomorrow at the playground of the former Jewish school in Dortmund on Zweite Kampstraße to have your papers checked."

We stared at one another. We had no idea what the order meant and tried to pump him for more information. "Will we be coming back to the site? Do we have to take our work clothes with us?"

"Here are your travel passes from the Dortmund Gestapo," he replied curtly.

The following day we took the train from Korbach to Dortmund and presented ourselves at the Kampstraße address. There a Gestapo official called us up by name and told us: "You're all under arrest. Anyone who tries to escape will be shot."

Together with other acquaintances, including friends from the vocational training school, we got into the trucks that had been driven up to the playground. All the while, the Gestapo men kept repeating their threat. Before the drivers started their engines, the guards told us that they had informed our relatives as to our whereabouts and that our families would be joining us the next day.

We rode to the Brakel section of Dortmund, where the Gestapo locked us in the ballroom of the Zum Deutschen Haus hotel.

The large ballroom was completely empty; there were no tables or chairs, not even blankets. We were forced to make ourselves at home on the bare floor. Personally, I didn't find this particularly hard to do— I was young and had already been sleeping on a straw mattress for two years. However, among the people who kept trickling in there were pregnant women, old and sick people, children and babies—most of the Jewish population from the area of greater Dortmund.

An anxious night followed.

The next day the Jews living outside Dortmund were brought in. Ernst and I hoped that our parents wouldn't be among them. A farmer, a friend of ours, had once offered to hide part of our family if the Nazis began arresting Jews. When we discovered that our parents were among the new arrivals, we reacted with surprise and anger. I berated them both, but our father was adamant: "We couldn't possibly leave you children alone."

We looked for a place in the ballroom, where in the meantime about a thousand people had been packed into a very confined space. No sooner had my parents finished telling us about the police officials in Schmallenberg who had taken them to Brakel than Ernst and I chided

ourselves for our own naïveté—we had voluntarily gone to Dortmund, without any police escort, "to have our papers checked."

Many of the people who had been deported to Dortmund from the
not exactly small district of Arnsberg arrived in broad daylight under
local police escort. All the nearby residents and passersby who wanted
to could see exactly what was happening.

My parents had been told that they would be resettled in Poland.
Each person was allowed to take fifty kilograms of luggage. So my parents had packed things for Ernst and me. My mother asked us anx-
iously whether we were hungry and gave Ernst and me some of the
food she had brought with her. Happy to get something into our stomachs again—we hadn't gotten anything to eat since our arrest on
Kampstraße—we sat down on the cold floor and began chewing and
observing what was going on around us. Gestapo officials in plainclothes and policemen in blue and green uniforms were guarding the
ballroom. The atmosphere was totally chaotic. As conditions became
increasingly unbearable, some of the representatives of the Jewish
community who had been charged with looking after us summoned
the courage to ask the Gestapo for permission to get mattresses for the
sick and the elderly from Jews' apartments that were no longer occupied. Shouting, the Nazi officials emphatically turned down their
request.

Only after much pleading were we able to wring permission from
the Gestapo to fetch straw from a nearby barn. Standing in one corner
of the ballroom, we handed out the straw to the old, the sick, and the
very young. Still, we couldn't raise people's spirits. They were restless,
unsettled, and frightened about what would happen next. No one
knew for sure what to expect, but many suspected the worst.

In Cattle Cars to the East

"Everyone out of the ballroom!" The bellowing Gestapo men roused
even the recently arrived Jews who had just dozed off from exhaustion.
The date was 1 March 1943, the time 8:00 A.M.

Before the Gestapo and the police cleared the ballroom, we had to
surrender all our valuables; each person was allowed to keep only
10 reichsmarks. We didn't have any more gold or silver, of course. But
after Kristallnacht my father had bought a seal ring with a good-carat

stone in it. During the general confusion he slipped it into Ernst's hand. "Hide it well. Someday it may be your ticket home."

Believe it or not, we managed to smuggle the ring through the various checkpoints. On Hellweg Street in Brakel—once again in broad daylight—the Jews boarded streetcars and rode to Ostentor (Eastgate). From there they walked about a kilometer to the South Station.

Ernst and I stayed behind with ten or fifteen other young people. The Gestapo had detailed us to load the luggage onto waiting trucks. After we had finished loading about two-thirds of the suitcases, bags, and packages, the Gestapo issued an order: "Get into the trucks! Come on, get going!" The few who had the courage to mention the fact that there were still suitcases and bags in the ballroom were simply ignored and shooed into the trucks with us.

When we reached the South Station the train—its locomotive belching steam—was ready to depart. After tossing the luggage into the last two railway cars, we rushed over to our father, who was calling and waving to us from one of the other cars. The train consisted almost exclusively of a line of cattle cars—except for a coach to accommodate the guards. No sooner had we climbed on to join our relatives and friends than the Gestapo bolted the doors behind us, and the train began to move.

The interior of the car was so dark that during the first few moments we were unable to make out anything. No more than a sliver of light was coming in through narrow openings near the roof of the car. First, we became aware of bodies pressing against us. Then our eyes got used to the half-light. Around seventy people had to find places for themselves. There was a lot of pushing and shoving as we sought to come to grips with the situation. We tried to sit in each other's lap one behind another, but somebody was always tripping over someone else trying to get to the pail in the corner that served as a toilet. In the beginning the women took pains to preserve their modesty and asked their husbands to hold a blanket up in front of them. The conditions were intolerable.

A good two hours later the train stopped in Bielefeld. When the doors were opened I recognized some young people from the vocational training school among the Jews who had been assembled at the station. I seized the opportunity with both hands and leaped out, which wasn't exactly what our guards had had in mind. The Dortmund police immediately drove me back.

I was bewildered. During the few seconds I was outside, I noticed something that made me suspicious. Since I didn't want to worry the others—especially my mother—I approached my father and whispered to him that the last two cars carrying our luggage were no longer connected to the train. "Where we're going," he replied in a low voice, "we won't be needing any luggage."

Ernst had heard my father's reply, too. So both he and I kept asking him what he meant. And for the first time he broke his silence about his time in Sachsenhausen. A few words spoke volumes: "The creatures we saw there weren't human beings—they were sadists. They treated us like animals. They drove us around like a herd of cattle, whipping us through the camp."

The train's next stop was the Silesian Station in Berlin. I was just able to make out the name through an opening in the side of the car. Father's only comment was: "Just as I thought—we're heading east." After a short stop the train continued on its journey.

The time seemed to drag on forever. People could barely move. The narrow openings didn't let enough air in; it was hot and muggy. We were gasping for breath. The pail in the corner had long since become inadequate.

The longer the journey lasted, the more unbearable the conditions inside the car became. Completely listless, my mother spent most of the time leaning against the side of the car; she no longer responded when we spoke to her.

By the second day our food supply had run out and, what was worse, there wasn't anything to drink. It was nearly impossible to quiet the children; they kept screaming and crying. The adults were tormented by thirst as well. The few who wanted to drink their own urine triggered some heated exchanges. The atmosphere was strained. Many people became aggressive and hysterical; arguments erupted and people shouted at each another. The train just kept moving relentlessly east.

Some elderly people died in the cattle car. . . .

Forgive me, but I'm simply unable to describe everything that happened.

The End of the Line—Auschwitz

After three days and three nights the train stopped at a place that was completely unfamiliar to us. It was late in the evening. I peeked out

and described to my father what I could see of the surrounding area—
a big patch of ground, watchtowers, a lot of barbed wire, and artificial
lighting as bright as day. In a low voice he told me: "We're in a concentration camp."

As people grew agitated they tried to reassure one another. "Things
won't be that bad." "Keep calm."

There were just a few minutes left for Father to tell us the whereabouts of important papers and objects of value. He concluded by saying: "I won't survive this; I'm too old. If the two of you do, go back to
Schmallenberg."

The doors of the cattle car flew open with a bang. A torrent of
shouts and yells descended upon us. "You Jew bastards! You swine!
Get down out of the car!"

SS men forced us off the train. Except for the dead and those who
were no longer able to move or lay motionless inside the cars, people
jumped or fell onto the brightly illuminated *Rampe,* or loading platform.[9] Over a thousand people crowded together, frantically trying to
shield themselves from the blows being rained down upon them by the
club-wielding SS men. Orders were yelled. "Men to the right! Women
without children to the left! Women with children to the left as well,
but in a separate group!"

Ernst and I held on to each other. We tried to stay together and ran
as fast as we could to protect ourselves from the hail of blows.
Hemmed in by the crowd, we had to stop at some point. We had lost
our parents—there had been no farewells.

SS men began sorting people out again. Men who were old or who
looked frail or unhealthy were directed to where the women and children were standing. I noticed two boys ahead of us whom I knew from
the vocational training workshop in Dortmund. They were ordered to
join the same group. I whispered to Ernst, "I'm going to make them
think I'm older."

When an SS man asked me what year I was born, I declared in a
booming voice that I was eighteen. He sent me to the right, to the
men's group.

I got into line next to Ernst, Max, and Emil Stern—my father's
cousins—and Max Rosenstein from Warburg. Rosenstein was holding a one-year-old child in his arms. We saw nothing unusual about
this—until all of a sudden the SS men discovered the child and one of

them rushed in our direction yelling at Rosenstein—hadn't he heard that children were to stay with their mothers? Rosenstein started to excuse himself. "My wife already has to take care of four little children and I just wanted to give her some relief. I . . . "

The SS man didn't listen to what Rosenstein had to say. He simply went up to him, snatched the child out of his arms, and walked off. Petrified, we saw him smash the child's head against the nearest pole. Rosenstein let out a scream and was about to rush over to his dead child, but we restrained him—the child was now beyond help. Many years after the war I would once again face the man who had murdered Max Rosenstein's child.

We were filled with fear and confusion as we stood on the *Rampe* at Auschwitz. Before we could really comprehend anything, trucks were brought up and the SS herded us onto them, yelling all the while. Everything happened so quickly that night—the night of 3–4 March 1943.

Monowitz

With about fifty other men we squeezed into one of the uncovered truck beds. The trucks raced off. The one we were in was traveling at such a high rate of speed that when it took the first curve, we were suddenly hurled to one side, and the vehicle nearly overturned. The driver brought the truck to a stop, and the next moment, our SS guards slammed their heavy rifle butts into us, driving us back to our places. After a short ride we reached a camp whose name we wouldn't learn until later: Auschwitz III–Monowitz.

"Get off! Get down! Get down!"

Ernst and I were standing near the end of the truck bed and jumped down, but anyone who didn't obey the order quickly enough was simply pushed off. Behind us people came crashing down, one on top of the other.

We were ordered to form two rows and run to a place where, in spite of the cold, we were forced to strip naked and throw our clothes onto a pile. Trying not to attract any attention, Ernst and I took the seal ring our father had given us in Brakel and hid it in the ground in hopes of retrieving it later.

To the accompaniment of more yelling and more blows, the guards drove us into a hut where SS men were sitting behind some tables. Prisoners wearing striped coats and trousers stood beside stools where we were ordered to sit down so that they could cut our hair—first the hair on our head and then our body hair. It was torture. The blades on the clippers were totally dull, so that the hair had to be pulled out rather than shaved off. It hurt like hell.

With our heads shaved, we stumbled over to the prisoners who had the job of tattooing an identification number on our arm. They spoke to us softly, inquired where we came from, and asked us in a friendly tone of voice to hold our arms still. They assured us that it wouldn't hurt and warned us never to forget the sequence of the numbers. It felt good once again to hear words spoken by friendly human beings. I was given number 104920, my brother number 104921.

Immediately afterward we had to report the numbers to the inmates who were responsible for registering us. When asked about our occupation, Ernst and I said we were locksmiths, even though we had only completed a course to prepare us to be trained in the trade. Later, our claim to be locksmiths turned out to be a kind of life insurance.

The registration process was the last time we were ever asked to give our names. From that point on, we no longer had names; we were just numbers.

Then came the shower room, where we were exposed to yet another indignity associated with camp life—the water was either boiling hot or ice cold. We were given neither soap nor towels and were dripping wet when we were thrown our striped prisoners' uniforms. Practically nothing fit—the uniforms were either too large or too small. So we had to exchange many pieces of clothing with one another before we were more or less properly dressed.

A short time later a prisoner appeared wearing an armband with the designation "Block 10." Almost in a polite tone of voice, he asked us to follow him. It turned out he was the block chief *(Blockälteste)* in charge of our new accommodations. These consisted of a long wooden barrack crammed with three-tiered bunks or pallets, each with a straw pillow and a blanket on top.

Before switching off the lights the block chief assigned us our bunks. No sooner had he left the dormitory and disappeared into a specially partitioned-off area in the front of the block than the inmates grew restless. Almost everyone began looking for relatives or friends;

people called out names—but seldom got a reply. Suddenly the room was bathed in light again; the block chief was standing in the doorway. "Listen to me, comrades!" he called out to us. After the inmates had settled down, he introduced himself: "I've looked at your registration papers and see that you all arrived here from Dortmund, my hometown. My name is Emil Meier. I come from the Lünen section of Dortmund and I've been in a number of concentration camps since 1933. You are now in Auschwitz, one of the biggest extermination camps ever built by the Nazis. The place you arrived is next to where the gas chambers are located. The relatives who are no longer with you are already dead."

We stared at him with disbelief. After a pause he went on: "There's only one thing left for us to do: We have to be determined to survive fascism."

Emil Meier turned off the lights again. That night, however, nobody thought about sleeping.

The First Day in the Camp

Around five o'clock the next morning we heard loud calls outside the barracks—"Coffee detail, fall out!" The block began to stir. The camp bell sounded and the light blinded our weary eyes. We struggled out of our bunks. While a few inmates left the block under orders to fetch the coffee, the barracks-room assistants (*Stubenältesten*) showed us how to make our beds. We had to straighten the straw mattresses until no lumps were visible. No matter how much we tried, we couldn't seem to smooth out all the clumps of straw. The more experienced inmates showed us newly arrived prisoners a trick: Start by pushing the straw in from the corners of the mattress. The checkered blankets had to be folded precisely and perfectly aligned with the bunks at the front of the barracks, near the door. The barracks-room assistant enjoined us to observe all the rules scrupulously. Otherwise we would have nothing but trouble with the SS.

After we finished making our beds we went to the washroom. Most of us pounced on the water faucets; for four days we hadn't gotten anything proper to drink. Inmates who had already been in the camp for some time tried to stop us. They pointed to the signs over the faucet that read "No Drinking Allowed! Danger!" and urged us not to drink.

Despite their warnings, some of the new prisoners thought the signs were just another example of Nazi chicanery and drank the water anyway. In a few days they contracted diarrhea and began to run high fevers. We quickly learned that in Monowitz this nearly always portended death.

We had only a few minutes to wash before we had to return to the block. There we were given a bowl and half a liter of ersatz coffee—a vile-smelling watery drink brewed from God knows what kind of leaves. But since our thirst exceeded our sense of revulsion, we gulped it down.

Around six o'clock Emil Meier led the entire block to a place where about twenty to twenty-five blocks consisting of 300 to 350 inmates each had assembled. He ordered us to form rows of five abreast and to stand rigidly at attention.

This was our first morning *Appell*, or roll call.[10] SS Blockführers responsible for three blocks each took a head count of the assembled prisoners and then accepted the lists prepared by the block chiefs. They signed the lists and passed them on to senior SS officers near the main gate. We were forbidden to speak during the procedure and tried to remain as motionless as possible. If an inmate swayed even slightly, he would be brutally beaten by the SS men.

After the inmates had been counted, an order was called out from the gate. "Head count tallies! Form up into Kommandos! Kommandos, move out!"[11]

That same day, Emil Meier took us back to the block and informed us that SS officials and employees of the nearby Buna works would be coming by to select suitable workers for the factory.[12] Meier told us that if we had learned a trade, we should by all means say so.

A short time later we were paraded slowly past members of the commission from I. G. Farben's Buna works. They sized us up and picked us out as if we were on exhibit at a slave market. Ernst and I once again said we were locksmiths. As soon as the Farben representatives had noted down our occupation, they left the block.

This was the first time since being deported from Dortmund that we felt somewhat at ease. We spent the rest of the day in the block. Emil Meier took the opportunity to give us more tips on how to behave. "Whenever you hear the SS shouting, walk in the opposite direction. Avoid any unnecessary contact with SS men! Whatever you do, don't look for family members in the camp or at your work site. That alone could give them an excuse to beat you up or beat you to death. You just have to accept the fact that those who aren't with you anymore are no longer alive. You mustn't continue to think that your relatives arrived here on an earlier transport and that somewhere, sometime, you're going to run into them—so whatever you do, don't start looking for them!"

As we stood at attention in the *Appellplatz* (roll-call square) in the evening, we watched the work Kommandos coming back through the camp gate—stooped, totally exhausted prisoners dragging themselves forward, many of them bearing collapsed and injured comrades or carrying the dead. They looked like walking corpses themselves. The inmates laid the dead on the ground beside the Kommandos, where they were counted along with the living. Anyone who had been counted in the morning had to be present in the square for the evening roll call—dead or alive.

That evening Ernst and I lay awake for quite some time. We tried to picture, however imperfectly, what was in store for us and encouraged each other to hold out for as long as possible.

Kommando 12

The next morning we went through the same routine again: the coffee detail, the latrine and washroom, the coffee line and the Appellplatz. That same day Ernst and I were assigned to Kommando 12. We reported to the Kommando directly after the roll call. Just as the Kommando was about to pass a group of high-ranking SS officers, an order rang out: "Caps off!" We removed them as fast as we could, stood at attention, our thumbs on our trouser seams, while the leader of the Kommando clicked his heels and made his report: "Kommando Twelve marching out with a hundred and twenty inmates."

After yet another head count, we paraded out of the camp with an SS escort, forced to sing as we marched. A hundred meters outside the gate, we passed a cordon of SS men carrying rifles and machine guns. Standing at intervals of fifty meters, they formed a chain of guard posts that enclosed the camp complex. It was called the *Postenkette*.[13] A short time later we entered a mammoth workplace—I. G. Farben's huge Buna synthetic rubber and petroleum facility, still under construction.

At the construction site of a power plant, the SS assigned us to a fore-man—not an inmate but one of the many civilian workers who were employed by the Buna works.

After Ernst and I assured the foreman that we were trained lock-smiths, he asked us if he was correct in assuming that we weren't prone to vertigo. Emil Meier had advised us always to answer "Yes" to any question. "Yes," he had told us, was usually correct, "No" was invariably wrong. So we replied in the affirmative.

The foreman then ordered us to climb thirty-meter-tall construction ladders and walk along steel girders no more than twenty-five centimeters wide. We tried our best not to be daunted by the height but were still shaky—though happy—when we reached the other end. The foreman must have decided that we would be of use to him, because he assigned us to work on the construction of the power plant's supporting structure. The girders were lifted with pulleys or a gigantic electric winch. Following a blueprint, we riveted, bolted, and welded the girders into place.

Extermination by Work

There were other companies besides I. G. Farben working on the factory grounds, including a number from the Ruhr. The construction site as well as the camp were surrounded by guard towers and barbed-wire fences. However, the barbed-wire fence at the construction site wasn't electrically charged because, besides the inmates, there were thousands of civilian workers employed there as well.

While we were working we had little contact with other people. During the day the only persons we encountered on the scaffold were other inmates, mostly Polish Jews. This posed a problem for *yekes* like us—that's what Eastern European Jews called German Jews—because the Polish Jews spoke only Yiddish. We tried to communicate with them using Lauschen-Kaudesch, the argot of Jewish livestock dealers, and *Mame-Luschen,* pidgin Yiddish.[14] But they constantly made fun of us until one day I had had my fill and grew angry: "Look, we're all in the same boat here, so let's stop this squabbling between German and Polish Jews." In time we got along quite well with one another.

The biggest advantage of our workplace was its inaccessibility—working high above ground, we had hardly any contact with the SS.

In other Kommandos, inmates suffered as a result of the arbitrary cruelty of the SS men and Kapos. Totally exhausted prisoners would often collapse and die as a result of the beatings meted out to them.

After a few weeks we were able to answer for ourselves the question we had constantly asked of older inmates at the beginning of our imprisonment, namely, how long can a person survive here? The answer was that if you couldn't get an easy work assignment, you couldn't even survive eight weeks. Certain Kommandos were to be avoided at all costs—for example, the transport Kommando, in which prisoners were forced to haul steel girders on their backs, dumped from freight cars a hundred meters away. To add to the prisoners' misery, the foremen would often order them to run instead of walk. The soil Kommandos were the worst of all: prisoners in these work gangs were made to dig ditches without having access to the proper tools. Then from a cable drum located about two kilometers away the cable Kommando laid cable in the ditches. The cable, approximately thirty centimeters in circumference and impregnated with bitumen, contained as many as 150 wires. The inmates in the cable Kommando simply couldn't make any headway with such a heavy load on their backs. Blows rained down upon them—so out of sheer necessity and with their last ounce of strength they somehow managed to pull the cable forward, millimeter by millimeter. The daily mortality rate in this Kommando was, of course, extremely high.

Max Stern, my father's cousin, was assigned to the cable Kommando. Within three to four weeks he had already become a *Muselmann*. At the end of one working day as we were preparing to march back to the camp, inmates in Max's Kommando informed us that SS men had beaten him half to death. Instead of surrendering his food bowl during work as ordered, he had hidden it under his coat. Coats had to be folded and laid on the ground and the SS would subsequently inspect them. They called out Max's identification number, beat him up, and tortured him for the next few hours while he was slaving away, until he finally collapsed.

Even though Max Stern wasn't in our Kommando, we carried him back to the camp with us. He was barely able to speak but somehow managed to show up for the roll call. After that we had no alternative but to take him to the infirmary. The next day we tried in vain to find out if he was still alive—but we never heard from him again.

Anyone who collapsed at work or tried to take it easy on the job was bullied, beaten, or kicked by the SS guards, the foremen, or the Kapos, many of whom were sadists and took pleasure in torturing their fellow inmates. The civilian workers not only witnessed these atrocities, from time to time they even participated in them. And they also knew about the existence of the gas chambers at Birkenau. When we spoke with the civilians, they asked us if we thought we would get out of the camp someday. We replied, "No one has ever stayed there for good" and then quoted the SS's macabre quip—"Everyone gets out, even if they have to leave through the chimney." Everybody in Monowitz knew what was going on. The civilian workers, it seemed, simply accepted the fact.

It took some time for a prisoner to learn how to get out of doing things. Of course, you also needed a good bit of luck. In the end, though, only a small number actually managed to escape extermination by work. I. G. Farben's Buna works expanded, and slave labor did produce results in the end.

Ernst and I were really quite lucky when it came to our work assignments. Compared to the grinding toil in other Kommandos, construction work wasn't that oppressive. Our Kapo, a political prisoner with a red triangle on his coat (part of the SS system of classifications applied to concentration camp prisoners), was a young Czech whom I guessed to be between twenty and twenty-two years of age. He never harassed us. Since he always gave us commands in Czech, I was surprised to learn one day that he was fluent in German. When I spoke to him about his knowledge of the language, all he said was: "I never want to speak that language as long as I live!"

Our work was anything but easy—the foreman wanted to see results and was very demanding. But in contrast to other Kommandos, in Kommando 12 an inmate could survive for quite some time.

The Evening Roll Call

In the late afternoon the SS began barking out orders at the construction site: "Foremen, Kapos, fall in!" We always had to stop working in time to return to the camp before nightfall. In the assembly areas at the work site the Kapos checked to make sure that they could account for those who had marched out of the camp in the morning regardless whether they were dead or alive. Those who had been beaten or had collapsed were carried back. We often had a number of exhausted or injured prisoners in our Kommando; however, it was rare for someone to be killed. After the Kapos had accounted for their charges, the SS issued the command: "Head count tallies! Fall in!"

Although we were totally exhausted after a long day's work, the SS would often force us to help carry building materials to the prisoners' camp that was then under construction. Sometimes we had to fill our caps with sand, and from time to time we had to help transport bricks. We greatly feared those evenings. The distance from our workplace to the camp was about one kilometer and most of us could barely stand. So three bricks quickly became an unbearable burden.

If the head count were off after the inmates had been assembled in the evening, the SS would comb the building site. Almost always they would discover a prisoner who had died abandoned and forgotten. What truly terrified us, though, was when someone was in fact missing. In that case the abuse and attempts at intimidation would begin when we marched through the main gate on our way back to the camp. After nearly everyone had been frisked, we were made to stand for hours on end in the Appellplatz, where the SS took one head count after another, adding and readding the figures. So long as the number of inmates didn't tally with the numbers on their lists, we were issued the following order: "Camp inmates will remain standing at attention!"

Standing motionless while it was cold and rainy was an indescribable torture. The hunger that gnawed at our exhausted bodies inspired the SS to devise a unique form of villainy. They ordered an uncovered kettle of soup to be brought up and had it placed two meters in front of us. Even if the soup was watery, the aroma still assailed our nostrils. As soon as the soup was cold, they would have the kettle hauled away.

As night fell the SS searched all the nearby villages, every car, anything that moved. We would often have to stand for the roll call all night long until we received the usual order in the morning: "Kommandos, move out!" Deprived of sleep, food, and drink, we were forced to go back to the construction site.

After roll calls like these there would be countless bodies lying on the ground. Many inmates simply had collapsed, and those who were too exhausted to go on tried to make a dash for the electrified barbed-wire fence.

Only a few ever actually reached the fence, because the SS men in the watchtowers started shooting as soon as a prisoner crossed the wire that had been stretched across the ground in front of it. In this way the guards saved themselves a lot of work, because when a prisoner succeeded in electrocuting himself and became entangled in the barbed wire the morning roll call took longer. Before the electricity could be turned off, people had to wait until it got light again and the guard posts around the perimeter of the camp had been reinforced. The work gangs standing at attention in the Appellplatz couldn't move out until the dead prisoner had been extricated from the barbed wire and the electricity had been turned back on. Only then could the daily routine proceed as usual.

Nighttime

After the evening roll call, which invariably took longer than the twenty- to thirty-minute morning roll call, we had only had a little time before the camp bell sounded and the lights were turned off.

Before lying down on your bunk to sleep, you had to secure your things, because a lot of stealing went on inside the blocks. You would put your shoes, any leftover bread, your spoon and food bowl—all your important belongings—under your head as a kind of headrest. If you didn't, they'd be gone the next morning.

For those who had to urinate at night, there was a pail at the front of the barracks, near the door. When the pail was full, the next person to use it had to empty the contents in the latrine. This was a job that everybody did his best to avoid, because it was quite a chore to carry a twenty-liter bucket down wooden steps through the mud. Since my brother and I slept near the front of the barracks, we learned in time to tell by listening how full the bucket was. Sometimes we were able to hold our urine just long enough for us to escape that unpleasant duty.

Many prisoners suffered from diarrhea, which was widespread throughout the camp. They had no alternative but to make the arduous trek to the latrine at night. After they opened the barracks door they had to call out to the watchtower—"Inmate number 104920 requests permission from the guard to relieve himself." An inmate could use the latrine only if the guard allowed him to do so. And then it was always important to be quick, because if the guard changed his mind while a prisoner was in the latrine or felt that the visit was taking too long, he would fire a few warning shots and yell "Out! Back to the block!"

On the way back the prisoner had to report to the guard again. "Inmate number 104920 returning to the block."

Although there was always a modicum of noise in the block at night—if someone wasn't going to the latrine, someone else was coughing or groaning—we nonetheless got used to sleeping during the five or six hours that were allotted to us.

After being in Monowitz for about a month, we ran into Rolf Goldschmidt after the evening roll call. He was sitting on his bunk in the row next to ours. He seemed very despondent and was mumbling to himself. "I can't stand it any more. I don't want to live." We tried to cheer him up, but it was hopeless.

We heard him get up at night. We were quite concerned. "Where are you going, Rolf?" we asked.

"To the latrine."

"Are you really going to the latrine?"

"Yes!"

I heard him call out to the guard and walk down the wooden steps. Half a minute later I heard gunfire. Rolf Goldschmidt had been shot dead while trying to throw himself onto the electrified barbed-wire fence.

Ede Besch

Many of the inmates in Block 10 died within a few weeks after their arrival in the camp. The empty bunks were soon filled with new prisoners. The fewer than seventy survivors from among the more than five hundred men from our transport were transferred to Block 8.

As we entered our new block I observed that the front row of bunks was still empty, so I unobtrusively placed myself next to them. In this way Ernst and I managed once again to secure the first couple of bunks in the barracks. The new block chief introduced himself as Ede Besch.

During the next couple of days I noticed that Ede was watching me. On my third day in the barracks he approached me after we had received our rations. "Come with me," he ordered.

I followed him to the partitioned-off area in the barracks where the block chiefs had their own beds, tables, and chairs. He started to look for something and then suddenly flung my registration card across the table. "There's something wrong here. Don't you notice something about this card?"

"No—should I?" I replied innocently.

"How old are you?"

"It says right here when I was born."

He looked at me sharply. "My dear Hänschen. I know a little about people—and I know you're not as old as it says on this card. Now tell me how old you really are."

I must have looked pretty embarrassed and scared because he tried to bolster my courage. "You can tell me the truth. I'm on your side. I try to keep people alive here. Now how old are you?"

"I was born in 1926," I admitted.

"Well, now that makes sense."

One or two weeks later Ede Besch sent for me again to ask about what kind of work I was doing. I told him about Kommando 12. Then he asked me whom I worked with and I told him about the other prisoners, the few civilian workers, and the foreman.

"Have you ever tried to engage Poles or ethnic Germans (*Volksdeutsche*) in conversation?"[15]

"Yes, we sometimes talk to each other, but mostly just in passing."

He then got to the heart of the matter. "Look, someone who has the courage to try to pass himself off as older on the *Rampe* surely has enough courage to do something that's against the camp rules."

I hesitated. "If it doesn't cost me my life, I guess I can do it."

Ede ended the conversation that evening on a positive note. "I'll be observing you a little while longer. And maybe I'll send for you one of these days."

Prisoners were used to do much of the administrative work inside the camp. When Ernst and I were sent to Monowitz in March 1943, it was largely political prisoners who were responsible for supervising the inmates who performed administrative tasks. Although some "greens" still occupied influential positions, prisoners who had been in the camp for quite some time told us that the situation had improved markedly since they had arrived.[16] In the past, they said, there had been a number of brutal and corrupt thugs among these criminal prisoners. Nonetheless, it was vital within the first few weeks for a newly arrived inmate to find another prisoner who had enough influence to provide him some support and protection against the criminal prisoners.

Prisoner-functionaries such as Emil Meier and Ede Besch were unable to improve working conditions in the harshest Kommandos, but they could secure individual prisoners a place in another Kommando. They could, for example, go to the Kapo of Kommando 12 and persuade him to take a particular prisoner into his work detail—but it was impossible for them to help everybody. It was only because of the help we received from Emil Meier and Ede Besch—and the good fortune of having been assigned to Kommando 12—that Ernst and I managed to survive for more than two months. After that, we were considered "veteran" prisoners. It was common knowledge that anyone who had an identification number under 200000 in the summer of 1943 had been in the camp for quite some time already and had demonstrated the will to live.

The SS

We also had something else in our favor that helped us survive: We understood German, the language of the camp. When the SS men started bellowing, we knew immediately what they were talking about. But many other inmates were brutally beaten simply because they couldn't understand a word of what was being said. Most of the dangerous confrontations with the SS took place in the morning and in the evening as we marched to and from the Buna works. As soon as we passed the chain of guard posts enclosing the camp, the SS would look for a recently arrived inmate to victimize. They could generally tell a newcomer because of his clean clothes and his shaved head. They would remove his cap, throw it over their shoulder, and issue an order: "Pick up your cap!"

The loss of one's cap could entail the severest punishment. While desperately trying to retrieve a discarded cap, a prisoner would often be shot dead "while attempting to escape." Anyone who had been in the camp for a while knew that any SS man who shot a prisoner "while attempting to escape" got three days' leave, twenty cigarettes, and a quarter-liter of schnapps. Veterans of the camp like us benefited from past experience. We never rushed to retrieve our caps, because we knew that we could quickly replace a "lost" cap by taking one from a dead or dying prisoner. And when marching five abreast we made sure that we were in the middle of the row, where we had more protection from the blows being rained down upon us by the SS.

It wasn't very hard to avoid running into the SS inside the camp, because they rarely spent any time there. At nightfall there were a few *Lagerführers* who patrolled the grounds.[17] And when there was a camp lockdown, twenty to thirty SS men might be assigned to ride up and down the blocks on bicycles or motorcycles to check for any prisoners who remained outside. Otherwise, we saw the SS only during roll calls. In the daytime, of course, while we were away at work, SS men would enter the camp to create pretexts for harassing us later. They found it entertaining, for example, to come into the barracks and rumple up our bunks and then accuse us in the evening of not having made them properly. They would not only withhold food from us as a form of punishment, they would also force us to do "punishment drills." Several SS *Rapportführers* would appear in the block, order the prisoners to line up, and shout at them nonstop: "On to your bunks! Under your bunks! Faster!"[18] Those who weren't quick enough would be hit with a truncheon. The only thing that energized our exhausted bodies and gave us the strength to cope with these "exercises" was the fear of being killed. Nevertheless, after just a few minutes the first prisoners would collapse and the SS men would proceed to beat them. It was only when the SS men lost interest in these kinds of "games" that they ordered us to make our bunks "properly," threatening to return in an hour to check up on us again. Although they usually didn't reappear, waiting for them to come back and continue their harassment wore many inmates down, especially the newly arrived. After I had been in the camp for a while, I knew enough to make a dash for the back of the barracks, to the last row of bunks, whenever such "drills" were about to take place. Since the SS didn't have an unobstructed view of the entire length of the barracks, it was easier to hide from them there. Beating such a hasty retreat, however, had one disadvantage: the dust I kicked up in the process nearly suffocated me.

We also expected to be harassed whenever the SS felt like having a soccer match in the Appellplatz—either among themselves or against prominent prisoners such as the block chiefs and the Kapos. When we returned to the camp in the evening and saw that goalposts had been set up in the square, we knew for certain that a game was in the offing.

And we also knew that the next thing the SS would do would be to order prisoners to dry the filthy wet square. After the roll call they would issue the following order: "Head count tallies—right face, left face—Blocks One to Ten, halt!" If you couldn't duck into another block quickly enough, you knew you were in for it. The SS would order ten entire blocks of prisoners to crawl across the square on their bellies a total of two or three times. The result, of course, was a dry soccer field.

The abuse didn't end there, however. We were also ordered to show up the next morning in clean prisoners' fatigues. The inmates immediately raced to the washrooms, trying desperately to scrub their clothes with any brush or primitive aid they could lay their hands on. The following morning the prisoners' uniforms were still wet but more or less clean.

Buttonholes, Shoes, and Cement Bags

Prisoners' clothing was made of light denim. Only on rare occasions did a prisoner have the good fortune of being issued fatigues made of heavier fabric. In fact, prisoners were often issued blue-and-white-striped coats that had only one sleeve—and sometimes no sleeves at all.

A missing button could become a matter of life and death, because the SS checked from time to time to ascertain whether a coat with six buttonholes actually had six buttons. A prisoner was in peril if he couldn't produce all the buttons he was supposed to have. To play it safe and avoid a flogging, we got hold of some thin wire to secure the buttons as firmly as possible so we wouldn't lose them.

The prisoners in our transport were allowed to keep their own shoes. Apparently the directors of I. G. Farben realized that laborers like us couldn't do their jobs in the Buna works without proper footwear. Most of the other prisoners in the camp were issued clogs, and within a few days their feet were sore and bloody. Shoes were a priceless possession, because if you ruined your feet, you couldn't walk properly. And if as a result you weren't fully capable of working, you were soon considered "superfluous." I wore out my own shoes first. And then I stole another pair. I came across a dead prisoner who may have been in the camp for all of two weeks. When I saw his body I had only one thought in mind—get those shoes. I quickly removed them, placed my old shoes next to him, and put on the new pair. Dead bodies were no longer anything out of the ordinary to us; we really couldn't care less about them. If you thought a body might be that of a friend, you would turn it over with your foot just to make sure.

Though I couldn't complain about my shoes, I, like everyone else, suffered from the weather in Auschwitz. For four months a year the sun was unbearably hot, and during the remaining months it either rained or snowed. Most of the time the mist that lay over the countryside was so thick that the SS wouldn't allow us to leave the camp for fear that we might try to escape. Several times a week during certain seasons, we had to remain standing after roll call and wait for the mist to clear. To make up for the time lost we were forced to work Sundays.

It didn't matter if it was foggy or rainy—by the time we returned from work in the evening, we were soaked to the skin. If we were still dripping wet when we queued up to get our food ration, the block chief would allow us to remove our clothes while we were still in line. There never seemed to be enough time for our fatigues to dry out by the following morning. So the next day we froze in our wet, clammy uniforms. Our resistance was so low that many of us contracted pneumonia and died.

One way we tried to keep ourselves dry was to use empty cement bags. We tore out the inner liner, which still had some cement stuck to it, made a hole at the top, put the bag on, and wore it under our uniforms. The dry paper also provided a little warmth.

After a while the SS caught on to what we were doing. The guards then made a game out of walking up to prisoners while they were slaving away and tapping them on the back with a stick. If a guard heard the rustle of paper, you knew you were in for it. After receiving your punishment, you could no longer tell whether your clothes were wet or dry.

The cement bags were stacked at the bottom of the power plant's supporting structure, near the winch. We hauled them up the scaffold, where we put them on under our clothes. We knew that the SS men were loath to expose themselves to the dangers of climbing around the top of the scaffold. But the same work site that proved to be such an advantage in the rain and fog turned out to be a peril in the frost and snow of winter. The steel girders iced over and got so cold that our hands froze to them. Since prisoners rarely managed to get hold of a pair of gloves, many of them lost fingers due to frostbite. And a number of them slipped and fell off the tall supporting structure.

Barracks-Room Assistants

I became Ede's auxiliary barracks-room assistant and later his junior assistant.[19] Unlike the senior barracks-room assistant, the junior assistant had to march out with the Kommandos in the morning. And in the evening he was only permitted to help carry out certain specific tasks, such as distributing bread and other food rations and cutting portions of margarine. Of course, I also had to shine the block chief's boots.

Sometimes Ede detailed me to work in the camp during the day. For example, he once ordered me to go with him to pick up bread: "Your only duty will be to watch how I count the bread! If you want to be the senior barracks-room assistant someday, you have to do exactly as I show you."

The four hundred men in the block would be given a hundred small loaves of rye bread. They were packed in baskets and handed out in the storeroom. Since there was only a single SS man present to supervise the distribution, the prisoners were ordered to do the counting in a loud and clear voice. We constantly kept our eyes on the SS man. As soon as he looked away from us and trained his sights on other prisoners, we would double the count: "Two, four, six, eight, eight, ten, twelve, fourteen, sixteen, eighteen, eighteen . . ."

After my initiation I often accompanied Ede. There was one time when the SS man caught me fudging the numbers. He ordered me to bend over a breadbasket and gave me ten blows on my buttocks. He used a kind of broomstick to beat me, but I was lucky. During official punishments in the Appellplatz, prisoners were slung over a sawhorse and flogged with a bullwhip. The first few lashes usually lacerated the skin.

After my punishment was over, the guard didn't pay any more attention to me. Apparently he thought the penalty he had exacted was sufficient to intimidate me. So I was able to continue double-counting.

Scrounging for food was a matter of life and death. Those who tried to subsist on the rations allocated to them soon became debilitated and died within a short period of time. Besides bread, our daily food ration consisted of ersatz coffee for breakfast, a bowl of soup for lunch, and a bowl of soup for dinner. In addition we received a tiny portion of margarine with each meal. Once every eight to ten days we were given a thin slice of cheese or sausage and on rare occasions a potato, which was usually rotten and foul smelling.

We were supposed to husband the bread we were given in the evening until the following morning. But that was impossible to do. We were so hungry that we were unable to keep ourselves from eating for that long. Besides, your stomach turned out to be the safest place to keep your ration from being stolen at night. Fights often broke out in the block when inmates were caught stealing bread from their fellow prisoners. In many cases the thieves would be killed by the prisoners on the spot. When people are near starvation, even the threat of death isn't enough to prevent them from stealing food.

I was even tormented by hunger while I was asleep. For instance, I once dreamed that a family we knew in Obringhausen in the Sauerland had cooked some potatoes and kohlrabi for their pigs and that I had leaped into the trough with the animals and gorged myself.

The morning and evening visits to the latrine offered prisoners an additional opportunity to obtain food and other items. The latrine became a regular commodity exchange where you could trade anything from buttons to wire to spoons. Garlic, onions, and tobacco, in particular, were in great demand. Although it didn't make much sense, many prisoners traded part of their bread ration for tobacco.

Although we felt hungry during the entire time we were in the camp, the food supply did improve slightly. Max Rosenstein, the inmate whose child had been murdered on the *Rampe,* had indicated during registration that he was a butcher and livestock dealer by trade. A few weeks after we arrived in the camp, a prisoner-functionary called out Max's number one evening and ordered him to report to the block chief. We were worried about what was going to happen to him. But he returned fifteen minutes later and told us that he had been detailed to work in the kitchen the next day and said he wouldn't forget us.

He rose from auxiliary assistant to become the prisoner in charge of filling the soup kettle and ladling out the soup. It was then that I decided to volunteer to get the soup kettles. Ede looked at me with surprise: "Why are you suddenly so eager to go and get the soup?"

Picking up the soup was a lousy job. You had to carry heavy kettles at a fast clip without spilling a drop while being supervised by SS men who were always ready to beat you. I explained to Ede that there was somebody working in the kitchen I knew and I wanted to let him know I was still alive.

No sooner had Max become aware of my presence than he told me always to bring two additional men along with me. From then on, ten prisoners from our block made the trek to the kitchen instead of the usual eight. And many times we returned with an extra kettle of soup.

Inequality pervaded the food distribution system, which was supervised by the barracks-room assistants. The prisoner who ladled out the soup made sure that the thicker, more nourishing contents from the bottom reached his best friends. During my time as barracks-room assistant I made it a point never to favor anyone. Before I started to dish out the soup, I gave the kettle a good stir with a long spoon to make sure that everyone would find a little piece of potato in his bowl. Cheating was a problem, however—even among the *Lagerältesten*.[20] In fact, even Ede Besch cheated. When the margarine was distributed, each prisoner was given a tiny cube from a big block. But it was the duty of the barracks-room assistant to first cut larger cubes for the block chiefs and the other barracks-room assistants. They were cheating their own friends, so what did it profit them in the end? At any rate, it was an inevitable part of the system.

The Commandant's Dog

The commandant of Monowitz, Heinrich Schwarz, would make a final inspection of the camp alone every evening. If he spotted a prisoner and thought, for whatever reason, there was something unusual about him, he would call the prisoner over, ask for his identification number, and write it down. The next morning the prisoner would have to report to the Blockführer. . . .

Schwarz had a German shepherd that was always romping around him but never strayed beyond a radius of a hundred meters. One evening when I was just about to go out the door and leave the barracks, Ede warned me: "That's Schwarz's dog over there."

"So what?" I said. "Hey, do you think we should try to catch it?"

Ede gave me a surprised look: "And then what?"

"Cook it on the grill."

"And just how do you plan to catch it?"

"Don't worry, I know a way."

"And how are you going to kill it?"

"Don't worry about that either."

"Leave me out of it. You'll have to take the responsibility," Ede muttered and disappeared into his room.

I opened the door a crack and whistled softly until the dog noticed me and began racing toward the barracks. When the creature jumped at the door, I opened it a little wider, grabbed its forelegs, and literally tore them apart. The dog died instantly.

In a flash I hid my quarry in a straw mattress at the back of the barrack. That night I got out of my bunk, borrowed a knife from Ede, and cut the dog's body up into six or seven pieces.

The next morning we hid the meat under an inmate's clothes and smuggled it out. During the day we cooked up a banquet. It was delicious.

The SS came into the camp with a large contingent of men to look for Schwarz's dog. They whistled and searched every corner of the grounds. They may have thought the dog had run into the electric wire. But they never imagined that someone might have enticed the animal into the barracks and dismembered it.

First Contacts with the Resistance

I had been Ede's barracks-room assistant for some time already when he talked with me one day about the contacts I had made at the Buna works. I told him about a civilian worker I had met there. His name was Jan Krupka, an ethnic German from Upper Silesia who spoke fairly good German. After I finished my report I added that Jan had "helped me send a letter to a cousin of mine in Germany."

"You did what?" Ede yelled. In the same breath, however, he asked me to give him all the details.

Jan's mother was Polish and he was not well disposed toward the Germans, which I discovered from a casual remark he had made. "You're not building this plant for the Germans; you're building it for us," he had muttered to himself. When I felt I could trust him, I told him about my "half Aryan" cousins Karl and Emil Friedrich in Schmallenberg.

"What do you want from me?" Jan asked suspiciously. After I explained to him that I wanted to write them a letter, he pointed to my striped prisoner's coat: "Do you want me to end up wearing that uniform, too?"

I asked him to take his time and think it over. Three or four days later Jan came over to me and told me to write the letter. Ernst got us an empty cement bag. Since it didn't have any cement stuck to it, we tore out the middle liner and used it as writing paper. I borrowed a pencil from Jan and slipped into a corner where nobody could see me and started writing: "This letter is coming via a person who means well by us. We're in a concentration camp. Auschwitz is an extermination camp. Except for Ernst and me there is nobody here from Schmallenberg who is still alive. Many people die here every day, and new transports arrive daily carrying people who are killed immediately. If Jews are being murdered, half-Jews will also be sent to Auschwitz. So go into hiding! Try to disappear somewhere so that you no longer officially exist. Otherwise you'll end up here, too."

At the end of the letter I made a big request: "Please see Daniel Marburger. He still has our father's gold watch. Trade it for some bread at the König Café, and mail the bread to the sender of this letter."

I had written Jan's exact address on another piece of paper.

"Well?" Ede broke in as I was explaining. "Did he send the letter?"

"Yes."

"Have you gotten an answer?"

"No."

Ede made a few more comments indicating his concern. A few days after our conversation, however, three loaves of bread showed up on the winch—but without any letter. Ernst and I immediately devoured them—first because we were hungry and second because we were afraid somebody from I. G. Farben would find the bread and use it to prove that we had had contact with the outside world. That would have meant certain death.

That same day, I went to see Ede: "I got an answer."

"How's that? What did they write?"

"They didn't write anything. They sent three loaves of bread."

As he was about to ask where the loaves were, I pointed to my stomach.

After the business with the bread, Ede named three prisoners and asked if I knew them. I said that I did. They were all members of the Resistance in Auschwitz.

"When they come up to you and shake your hand," Ede instructed me, "accept whatever they have to slip you and take it to the construction site. Give it to Jan Krupka. You don't have to give him a long explanation. Just say: Pass this on to the Resistance on the outside." The system worked perfectly—every other day we were able to get a message out.

The Resistance

Ede was extremely agitated: "We've got to get a secret message out to London. Security is a top priority, and it has to get there the fastest way possible. We need your friend Krupka to help us. So get a move on!"

I carried out my orders at once, but it took me three days before I could summon the courage to ask what the message contained.

"Maps of Birkenau," Ede replied. "The railway lines, the crematoria, everything drawn in minute detail, along with a plea to bomb the crematoria, the gas chambers, and the railway lines."

On another occasion I was sent to Birkenau on a scrounging expedition.

"What do you want me to look for?"

"Rings, gold, and so forth. . . ."

A Polish Jew who was involved in the Resistance was present at our meeting. He turned to me and said: "And bring some *lokshn* back with you."

I knew *lokshn* was the Yiddish word for noodles. That much I had picked up. "Noodles? Why noodles?"

"You dumb *yeke. Lokshn* means dollars."

"OK, I guess I've just learned something new."

"But get the hard ones, not the soft."

I looked at him in amazement: "What's the difference between hard and soft *lokshn*?"

"American gold pieces—that's what we want you to get!"

After the Jews disembarked from the trains, the Little Red Riding Hood (*Rotkäppchen*) and Little White Riding Hood (*Weißkäppchen*) Kommandos sorted the contents of their luggage on the loading platform. Both of them were women's Kommandos. The better items were reloaded onto the trains, sent back, and distributed to Germans as donations from the Winter Relief Agency (*Winterhilfswerk*). In reality, of course, they were the property of Jews who had been deported to Auschwitz and murdered there. The so-called "Canada" Kommando took charge of whatever remained of the dead Jews' belongings.[21]

After a scandal involving SS men who were getting rich off looted Jewish property, the SS could no longer afford to steal valuables from the *Rampe*. The Resistance saw to it that the SS stopped scrutinizing prisoners whom they took to Birkenau with them so that to some extent we were able to move about freely. Since the SS kept a precise list of everyone who left the camp, you just had to make sure that you returned on the same truck you had arrived on. In the meantime, we managed to get hold of clothing and valuables with which to bribe the SS. We would, for example, trade the SS a ten-carat ring for a sausage or a loaf of bread. Sometimes, albeit rarely, we even managed to get schnapps into the block. More often than not, though, all we managed to scrounge up was additional clothing for the inmates through our contacts in the Canada Kommando.

The political prisoners usually held discussions after the evening roll call. I was allowed to be present when they gathered in Ede's quarters. The Communists organized political training and sang songs in praise of socialism. Being young and politically naive, I listened with great curiosity to their debates. "You're socialists, aren't you?" I ventured to ask one day. "What's the difference between a Communist and a socialist?"

"Well, there are socialists, Communists, Bolsheviks, Stalinists, Leninists, and so forth. . . ." They rattled off the names, but their attempt to explain the differences didn't help me very much.

Prisoners who were in contact with the Resistance knew where the front line was. After the Red Army's victory at Stalingrad, news about the German retreat arrived in the camp and gave us fresh hope. We began to count the months and calculate how long it would take before we were liberated.

Sabotage

Sabotage whatever you can! Any little thing you damage or destroy will shorten the war and bring us that much closer to liberation.

The Communists attached particular importance to subverting production. So we tried as best we could to carry out acts of sabotage at the Buna works. Whenever representatives of I. G. Farben announced that they were going to visit Monowitz to inspect the facilities, the SS became very nervous. They were responsible for seeing that the prisoners were working properly and that the prisoner labor convoys arrived and left without any disruptions. No sooner did the SS learn of an impending inspection than the political prisoner-functionaries heard about it from their own sources.

One day we received news that Farben representatives were planning to inspect the power plant and conduct a test run of turbine no. 4. I passed the information on to Fred Salomon, a prisoner from Bochum who was employed in the electricians' Kommando. I had met Fred while I was studying at the vocational training school in Dortmund. He gave his assurance: "OK, I know just what to do. Don't worry—you can count on me."

On the day of the inspection we were perched on the girders of the support structure, where we could discreetly observe everything that was going on below. The distinguished visitors from I. G. Farben appeared at the power plant as announced. After they had finished delivering some high-sounding speeches, one of the technicians walked over to the large switch box, intending to demonstrate how powerful the turbine was. However, the moment he pulled the lever to activate the machine, there was a loud explosion. We saw a huge tongue of flame and lots of smoke; the smell of burned cables assailed our nostrils. Fred Salomon had made sure there was plenty of "cable salad."

Down below there was pandemonium. SS men were yelling everywhere; they wanted to know who had been working near the switch box. They selected prisoners at random and ordered them to report to the Blockführer that evening.

The SS hanged a number of inmates because of this act of sabotage, but they never found out who was actually responsible.

The Stonemason-Training Kommando

Prisoner foremen, Kapos, and block chiefs enjoyed certain privileges. Not only did they have their own quarters, they often wore handmade boots with reinforced toe caps and tight calf fittings that were made by Polish shoemakers in Auschwitz. I personally shined Ede Besch's pair quite a few times before he lost his position as block chief in the spring of 1944 because of the many liberties he had taken in dealing with the SS. SS men, for example, commissioned Polish Jews to knit socks for them. We inmates, by the way, generally wore footcloths because socks were such rare commodities. In any case, Ede approached the knitting Kommando on his own and ordered five pairs of socks for himself. When the SS came by to pick up their order, they found that it wasn't ready yet. In their defense, the prisoners in the knitting Kommando explained that they had been busy knitting five pairs of socks for the block chief in Block 8.

I remember that I was doing something or other in the block when the SS men, livid with rage, stormed in. They screamed at Ede, who pretended not to notice them: "Stand at attention! Where are the socks?"

"What socks?"

"You had the Jews knit socks for you. Where are they? They're ours."

It quickly became clear that it was useless for Ede to deny the fact. He removed his socks, took the other four pairs out of his locker, and gave them to the SS man who was standing closest to him. Another SS man then drew the long knife that SS men always carried with them, went up to Ede, cut his red armband in two, and ripped it off: "You've been block chief long enough. As of tomorrow you're detailed to a punishment company (*Strafkompanie*)!"[22]

Ede had the courage to talk back: "It's not up to you two to decide that." And this to a couple of SS men! As soon as we were alone again, I sat down next to him. "What's going to become of you now?"

Ede tried to calm me. "First, I'm going to see the top prisoner-functionaries, the senior camp prisoner (*Lagerälteste*) and the camp Kapo (*Lagerkapo*)."

Before the lights were turned off, he came back to the block briefly to tell me that he was going to slip off to the infirmary and stay there for a while. There he would be safe from the SS for the time being; the SS, he said, avoided entering the infirmary block for fear of contracting infectious diseases.

I was reassured when Ede returned four or six weeks later in a cheerful mood. "Have you ever been a stonemason?" he asked me.

"What do you want from me? I've only been on this earth a few years."

"Starting tomorrow I'm heading up a new Kommando—Kommando 326, a brigade to train stonemasons. It's made up mostly of Hungarian and Polish Jews. And effective immediately, you're my foreman."

"But I don't know anything about laying bricks."

"I'll teach you. Just show up there tomorrow."

While Ernst continued to work at the construction site, I ended up in the stonemason-training Kommando. We built brick walls using clay for our mortar and learned how to do the cross and the English bonds. After the walls had been appraised, they were torn down. Thousands of prisoners went through this twelve-week training course before I. G. Farben employed them as stonemason brigades (*Maurerkolonnen*) in the Buna works.

We realized that the job for which we were being trained was fairly tolerable. But the months we spent in the stonemason-training Kommando nevertheless turned out to be extremely depressing. The facility was located directly between the camp and the SS's living quarters. So we were forced to watch as SS men selected the most beautiful women on the *Rampe* at Birkenau, took them to their compound, held a nightlong orgy, and then sent them back the next day—to the gas chamber.

The Infirmary

It was harder to get into the infirmary than to arrange for an audience with the pope. The infirmary block was guarded by SS men and separated from the rest of the camp by an electrified barbed-wire fence. If an inmate did get in, however, the infirmary was a temporary haven. Because of the danger of contracting typhus, no guard ever ventured into the facility.

Prisoner-physicians managed the infirmary, and there was no shortage of good doctors. New physicians arrived every day with the transports. The help they could offer was minimal, however, since there wasn't enough dressing material or drugs. Wounds were dressed with crepe paper. The few drugs to which the doctors had access had been smuggled into the camp with the help of partisan bands. The doctors tried their best to help the sick. But after two weeks of treatment, SS physicians would conduct a selection and send patients who were still unfit for work to the gas chamber.

My brother had been in the infirmary for ten days with jaundice when Ede came to see me after the evening roll call: "Is your brother still in the infirmary?"

"Yes. Why?"

"Make sure that he's out of there by tomorrow morning. There's going to be a selection."

I knew that I had to warn Ernst, but it was difficult for an inmate to get past the guards. In my first attempt, I said that I had some business to take care of in the infirmary, but I wasn't convincing enough. The SS man—his name was Neubert, but I didn't find that out until long after the war—grew suspicious. He beat and kicked me and chased me away.

I waited impatiently until another SS man was finally sent to relieve him later that evening and tried my luck again. This time I succeeded. I rushed over to my brother's bed and whispered: "Get yourself discharged tomorrow! It's imperative!" The next instant I was outside again.

Ernst understood immediately what I had meant. The following morning he went to the prisoner-physician and told him that he was feeling fine. He was discharged just moments before Dr. Fischer and his men came to make the selection.

If he hadn't gotten out of the infirmary in time, there's no question that he would've been selected and sent to the gas chamber.

Selection

Like most other prisoners, I had abscesses. Fortunately, though, I had them only on my legs. These pus-filled cavities were caused by a vitamin deficiency and were extremely painful. Since there were no antibiotics in the camp, we treated them ourselves by removing the contaminated tissue with a knife, tearing a shirt apart, and dressing the wounds with the torn strips of cloth.

One summer evening after the roll call I tugged at my brother's sleeve behind the block: "Come with me. There's something very wrong with my legs. I feel this incredible twitching down there."

I could barely summon the courage to undo the dressings, but with a little willpower we gradually managed to remove them. Horrified, we both stared at my legs—the wounds were crawling with maggots. Until then I could more or less tolerate the abscesses, but from then on it became harder and harder. It seemed as if I was rotting from the bottom up.

Every four weeks we got a Sunday off for "delousing," as the SS so nicely put it. Delousing, however, turned out to be nothing more than part of the selection process. After the roll-call bell signaled a block lockdown, we had to walk past a table where SS men were seated and present our registration cards. If you looked like a *Muselmann,* they would push your card off to the left. The next day after the morning roll call, the block chief would send the prisoners whom the SS men had singled out the day before back to the block. During the day a truck would pick them up and drive them to Birkenau. It was an open secret that anyone whose registration card ended up on the left side of the table would be gassed.

When the block lockdown was lifted on our Sundays off, we were allowed to walk anywhere in the camp. But what was there to see? Just a lot of pathetic-looking prisoners, many of whom kept repeating the same words over and over again: "I'm leaving tomorrow. My registration card was pushed to the left."

My legs got progressively worse and since I was in danger of being selected for gassing, I sought out Ede the Saturday before our next Sunday off: "This thing with my legs doesn't look good. Do you want to take a look?"

"No thanks. I can imagine what it looks like."

"If I have to go through the selection process, I know I won't survive."

He tried to console me: "Well, at least there's no selection today."

"I know, it's tomorrow," I replied impatiently.

"There are twenty-four hours until tomorrow. So don't get yourself all worked up now about tomorrow's selection."

On Sunday the roll-call bell sounded and I heard the block chiefs yelling: "Block lockdown! Everyone inside!" I hobbled over to Ede as quickly as I could: "The twenty-four hours are up. What are we to do now?" I was extremely nervous.

"Here's your registration card and the key to the broom closet. Lock it from the inside and don't come out until I tell you to."

Sweaty with fear, I survived in the little broom closet until Ede came to get me. The ruse worked. Fortunately, the SS didn't take a count before the selections, so Ede managed to hide my registration card on another occasion, too. He literally saved my life.

There was another way to save someone who had been selected. You could substitute someone else's registration card for that person's. There were instances in which people were saved in this way from being killed. But they had to spend the rest of their lives trying to cope with the fact that someone else had died for them.

It was in Auschwitz that I began to doubt the existence of God. Even though Jews were strictly forbidden to pray, Orthodox Jews nevertheless met in a corner of the barracks to pray in secret. I could understand the softly murmured prayers they recited by heart, but I didn't join them. Instead, I baited them: "That's the last thing you should be doing! There is no God! The things that are going on here," I said, pointing in the direction of Birkenau, "shouldn't be allowed to happen. Where is God?" When the religious Jews replied that we must have done something wrong, that God was punishing us, I let them have it: "Including four-month-old infants? They certainly didn't do anything wrong!"

Medical Experimentation on Human Beings

One day in the summer of 1944, some SS men came to see the barracks-room assistants. Unfortunately for me, I happened to be in the block at the time and not at work like the other prisoners.

"Open your mouth!" they ordered me.

My teeth were still in good condition, but it seems that a good set of teeth was precisely what they were looking for. They handed me a piece of paper that contained an order to "report to the dental clinic in the infirmary tomorrow morning by 9:00 A.M." They had already given the same order to ten or twelve other prisoners.

I had no alternative but to obey. The following morning, I presented myself at the infirmary. But instead of being taken to the primitive facility in which inmates normally went for dental treatment, I was led to a real dentist's office with an operating chair and all the other paraphernalia of a dental practice. I protested that I didn't have a toothache, but the SS men pushed me into the chair anyway and held me down while the SS dentist drilled one molar after another—without any anesthetic. Nor did he treat me very gently in the process.

After he finished packing the filling material into the cavities he had created, he told me to notify him immediately if I noticed any pain.

And, of course, two days later I experienced excruciating pain.

The dentist repeated the entire procedure. He drilled my molars again and inserted new fillings.

After every treatment the pain recurred. I was forced to endure these experiments two or three times more until January 1945.

The SS doctors were using us as human guinea pigs.

"After Us It's Their Turn!"

When we learned of the British and American landings in Normandy in the summer of 1944, we were overjoyed and took renewed courage. The news that Heinrich Himmler had ordered the SS to blow up the crematoria at Birkenau reached us at the end of the year. We were nearly euphoric, hoping that the selections would stop. The crematoria that were still intact were incapable of incinerating the persons who died "naturally." In the next few weeks, bodies began to pile up all over Monowitz.

The mood in the camp grew increasingly tense. The Resistance debated what to do next. It was rumored that the Germans might still try to kill us.

The Red Army had captured Warsaw and was at the gates of Kraków. If we kept quiet at night, we could sometimes hear the distant rumble of artillery. We used our fingers to calculate when Soviet soldiers would arrive at our camp and liberate us.

But nobody knew exactly what the Germans were planning. So three of our friends organized an escape, firmly convinced that the Germans were not going to leave anybody alive.

We thought that they had succeeded. But a few days later as we were returning from work, we saw them in the camp again. They were standing on a platform near the main gate, their bodies beaten black and blue, their eyes swollen shut, and a sign hanging from their necks reading: "We were free, but because it's so nice here, we've come back."

The gallows were awaiting them in the Appellplatz. We had

witnessed similar scenes before during our captivity, but this time we found it particularly horrifying.

While we were standing in line for roll call, I asked the person next to me as unobtrusively as I could where Fred Diament was. He was the brother of one of the three condemned prisoners. I was relieved to learn that he was in the infirmary. It gave the SS a certain joy to force a son, father, or brother to play the role of hangman during the execution of a relative.

After the roll call, SS men led our friends to the gallows. SS Rapportführer Rakers took up position directly below the men and, in the name of Reichsführer SS Heinrich Himmler, he read the death sentences: "The sentences will be carried out immediately."

Before other inmates had a chance to put nooses around the condemned prisoners' necks, the three men called out to us in booming voices: "Comrades, we are the last to be executed, so stay the course! After us, it's their turn!" This was the first time I had ever witnessed anything like this in Auschwitz. The SS men reacted instantly. They leaped onto the gallows, placed nooses around the men's necks, and kicked the stools from under them before they could yell anything else.

We stared straight ahead.

It was 15 January 1945 when the SS hanged three of our friends, thirteen days before the Red Army liberated Auschwitz, and three days before an event took place that none of us could have predicted.

The Death March

Late in the evening of 18 January 1945, around eleven or twelve o'clock, the camp bell sounded once again.

"All inmates fall out and bring one blanket with you!"

We assembled in the Appellplatz.

"Those who can't walk are to stay behind."

Although we thought anything was possible, none of us had imagined that the camp was going to be evacuated. Nothing had filtered down to us. And apparently even the SS hadn't been informed. We had never seen the guards so edgy before—they were actually more nervous than we were.

Since autumn, I had been having problems with my knee. It was inflamed and I could walk on it only with great difficulty. So Ernst and

I had to decide whether we should stay behind. Ultimately it was Ede who decided us: "It can't last that long. Wherever they make us go, I'm sure the Red Army won't be far behind."

For the first time, nobody took a head count in Auschwitz. Nor was there a roll call or anything resembling it. People were running around in a state of confusion. The SS men were frantically firing their guns into the air. When the main gate was opened, we ran out of the camp like a herd of wild animals.

The SS tried in vain to arrange us in columns five abreast. After marching just a few kilometers, the first inmates fell behind. On either side of the column, thousands of prisoners who had joined us from the satellite camps were pressing in on us. We had marched off from Monowitz with about nine thousand people. But during the night the column swelled to between thirty thousand and fifty thousand prisoners.

It was bitterly cold as we dragged ourselves through snowdrifts thirty to forty centimeters high. Within an hour, we heard the first gunshots. It didn't take long for us to realize that those who fell down or couldn't continue would be shot dead en route. Rapportführer Rakers was riding up and down the column in the sidecar of a motorcycle, shooting prisoners who had fallen behind. We tried to remain at the front of the column, because it was much more dangerous in the rear.

The SS men had taken part of their provisions along with them. But when they found that their knapsacks were too heavy on their backs, they stole horse carts and similar conveyances in the villages we were passing through and simply harnessed ten prisoners to them.

We marched throughout the night and the following day. Frankly, I was ready to give up. "I can't hold out with this knee. The pain is driving me crazy." Ernst and Ede got on either side of me and helped me along. They encouraged me to hold out and tried to cheer me up. During the evening of the second day a heavy snowstorm came up. It lashed our faces and made us feel as if someone were throwing sand or gravel into our faces. I couldn't go on. Icicles hung from our eyebrows and we shivered with cold. We were so weak that we didn't even have the strength to pick up a second or third blanket and carry it with us.

Around ten o'clock at night, the SS finally drove us into a brickworks near Mikolow. Exhausted, nearly everyone collapsed, pulled their blankets over themselves, and fell asleep. A few of us continued to talk in a whisper.

The next day we joined five other men and tried to get some rest while we were marching. The men who were walking in the middle of the line linked arms with those on the outside and were dragged along by them so that they could get a little sleep. After a while we switched positions. That's how we saved each other's lives.

On the evening of the second day the death march reached Gleiwitz (Gliwice), where some of the prisoners who were still alive were herded into a camp, while the rest were driven toward the railroad station, to a place that had a lot of sheds and boxcars.

We looked among the sheds for any place we could shelter ourselves from the wind. We were terribly hungry. We had long since eaten the half loaf of bread that we had been issued when we left Monowitz. As clever as always, Ede managed to get hold of some boiled pork from the SS. The SS butchered any live animals they could lay their hands on and cooked them up in huge pots. In spite of Ede's warning to be careful about eating too quickly, we plunged into the food.

During the days that followed, the prisoners were loaded onto trains. We decided to stay behind as long as possible, figuring that the Germans would eventually run out of rolling stock and locomotives. We hoped the approaching front would overtake us in time. However, the Germans managed to pack every last prisoner into the cars.

We were playing for time during the boarding process when misfortune struck. An SS man noticed that I was dawdling. He jabbed me with the butt of his rifle and hit my infected knee. I let out a holler and fell backward, but at the last moment some other prisoners grabbed my hands and pulled me into the car.

There were more than a hundred people crammed into the tender. Standing up, you could just peek over the side. The SS ordered us to get down, however, so we ended up perched on each other's laps one behind the other.

There was no change in the weather; it was still ice cold and snowy. We took the blankets we had pulled over our heads and spread them out as best we could so that they covered our legs. We tried desperately to stay awake at night so we wouldn't freeze to death. In the morning we carefully pressed the thick blanket of snow that had fallen the night before into clumps which we saved and nibbled on as needed. After a few days we hardly noticed our hunger anymore. Thirst, however, drove many people crazy. I saw people go mad and drink their own urine. But the salts in the urine only drew further water from their tissues and actually increased their desire for liquid.

During my journey into the unknown, my teeth started causing me pain again. My molars still contained the fillings that the SS dentist had put in them. Not knowing what to do, I turned to Ernst for help: "One way or another, these fillings have got to come out." Running our fingers along the side of the tender, we found a rusty nail. We bent it back and forth until we finally got it out. My brother then used it to break up the fillings and remove them.

People were dying on a massive scale. In the beginning, the frozen corpses were thrown off the moving train. As we got closer to Germany, however, the train stopped every morning and the bodies were placed in the first few cars, which had been cleared out to serve as a kind of morgue. Also, the nearer we got to Germany the more people began to harass us. Instead of throwing something to eat into the cars, they threw rocks and spat at us.

When we arrived in Germany after what seemed like an eternity, we found that the dead in the first few cars had been piled in heaps that were higher than the sides of the cars. More than half the prisoners hadn't survived the last few days of the journey.

It turned out, however, that the stop in Weimar wasn't the end of our odyssey. The Buchenwald concentration camp was filled to capacity and wouldn't accept any more prisoners. Despite frequent stops because of the many air raids, we nevertheless kept moving—but with no idea where we were headed.

The Cold Hell

On 28 January 1945, exactly ten days after we had marched out of Auschwitz, the SS deposited us at Nordhausen. Even to longtime concentration camp inmates, the name Mittelbau-Dora meant nothing.

We were immediately put to work. The combination of exhaustion and illness helped dim our memories of the first few days. We were forced to labor as locksmiths in an underground rocket factory. Trucks drove our Kommando to the northern tunnel entrance. We then walked 100 to 150 meters to reach our workplaces. Operating day and night with shifts of forced laborers, these subterranean factories turned out V-2 rockets around the clock. The "V," by the way, stood for *Vergeltung*—revenge.

Ede once again found a job for himself, so we didn't see him as often as we used to. But he looked in on us in the evening whenever he could and always brought us something to eat.

Rumors of sabotage circulated throughout the tunnels. Then one day more than ten out of thirty completed rockets were returned because their ignition systems had malfunctioned. The SS men screamed at us: "Sabotage, a deliberate act of sabotage! You're all going to be shot!"

From that point on, an SS guard was posted next to every other prisoner working on the assembly line. The guards were ordered to keep them under constant surveillance. If a prisoner so much as dropped a key into a rocket during the assembly process, he had to stand at attention and make a full report. Then the SS would start shouting "Sabotage!"

Prisoners who were suspected of sabotage would be strung up over a rocket in the main plant and hanged.

If Auschwitz was the hot hell, Dora was the cold hell.

At the end of February, the SS began closing off some of the smaller tunnels. There were rumors that the Germans intended to do something else with us. Ede told us of plans to transfer about a thousand people to the Boelke Kaserne (barracks) in Nordhausen and suggested we join them.

Prisoners called the subcamp at Nordhausen the Verreck Kaserne (death barracks) because anyone who was no longer fit for work was sent there to die. Since the camp was grossly overcrowded due to the constant arrival of new prisoners from the death marches, the Germans had to empty the warehouses in the barracks to make room for them.

Ernst and I reacted skeptically to Ede's suggestion. Another way to get transferred from the factory was to volunteer for a bomb disposal detail, but we weren't very eager to do that either. Then Ede told us he was afraid that we—the Jews—were to be gassed in the smaller tunnels: "At least if we're in Nordhausen, in the center of town, we'll have a better chance of surviving."

We agreed.

After some four weeks in the camp we got ourselves transferred to the Boelke Kaserne, where we were put up on the second floor of a former warehouse. There were no bunks, so we slept on the cold floor with just one blanket.

I could barely walk on my inflamed legs. The contaminated tissue in my wounds had grown well above the surface of the skin. The dressings no longer helped.

"Make sure to show up for the roll call today," Ede ordered, "and when it's over, turn around, walk back up the steps, and get under the blankets."

During the day the blankets were folded and stacked up. I crawled under them and slept or kept still all day long.

For the next few days I only got up to appear for the roll calls.

Ede got hold of a Jewish doctor, who examined my legs: "We can't do anything with the knee. You just need to rest. Normally we'd aspirate it. However, we do have to treat the abscesses."

When I naively asked what he intended to do, he explained: "This evening after work, you and Ede come down to our makeshift infirmary. The first thing we'll do is debride the granulation tissue."

I wondered whether he might cauterize the wounds. But no sooner had his assistants laid me on a pallet—two men sat on top of me and held me down—than I knew I had guessed wrong. The doctor removed the contaminated tissue with a scalpel. Gritting my teeth, I kept my mouth shut as best I could. However, after they had finished with the first leg I cried out: "That's enough! I can't take any more."

"Look, you're already here now. So we might as well go on."

"Don't you have some kind of anesthetic so I won't feel it as much? I can't stand the pain."

Then someone said, literally—and I'll never forget it: "Sure, we have an anesthetic. Where's the mallet?"

I said no thanks and just continued to grit my teeth.

The Escape

Nordhausen was bombed repeatedly during the early part of April. In the daylight hours of 3 April—the labor brigades hadn't returned yet—the Blockführer's compound, where the SS were quartered at the time, was demolished. "Well, so there's still some justice in the world," we muttered to ourselves.

The next day during the morning roll call, we heard the sound of approaching aircraft. We knew that after the fighter-bombers dropped their ordnance, they would strafe anything that moved. Frightened, we ran back to the barracks and rushed up the steps just as the first bombs hit with a deafening crash. Seconds later, the building in which we were standing was in flames. Ede yelled for us to follow him as he leaped out a window. After less than a moment's reflection, Ernst and I followed suit. I landed in a heap on the ground, stunned. As I looked around the yard I saw hundreds of people doubled up on the ground and ablaze. I was panic-stricken but managed to pull myself together. Ernst and I ran into an open field, threw ourselves into a bomb crater, and lay as flat as we could at the bottom.

The bombs continued to fall, when all at once I felt as though my leg had been torn off. Screaming with pain, I turned around and found that a huge clump of earth had fallen on the hollow of my bad knee.

When the air raid was over, everybody was in a state of total confusion. Keeping perfectly still, we watched as the SS rounded up the remaining prisoners.

We had lost track of Ede—he had disappeared for good.

After things calmed down, we worked our way out of the crater. On the way to Nordhausen we discovered a dead SS man under a bridge, his service pistol still in his holster. I ran over and grabbed it, but Ernst implored me: "Throw that thing away, throw it away!" He finally convinced me to leave the gun behind.

I remember that we had warm, freshly baked bread to eat in Nordhausen, but I can't recall if we had had to storm the bakery to get it—there were some escaped prisoners in the city—or if the baker had given us the bread voluntarily.

My brother and I had devised our own nonverbal language in the camp that was made up largely of facial expressions and head gestures. We continued to use it to communicate with each other even after we escaped. When we saw a sign that read "Kassel 75 km," we just had to look at each other and nod. That night we started walking through the Thuringian Forest in the direction of Kassel. We headed for the village where Herr Sauer lived. He was the butcher who had helped us once before.

During the three days we were on the run, we didn't see a soul. The only sound we heard was that of aircraft flying overhead. No sooner did we enter a clearing than we saw a bunch of rifles pointed at us and heard some gruff voices: "Get your hands up! Who are you?"

We were face to face with four elderly members of the Volkssturm.[23] We explained that we were concentration camp inmates, German Jews who simply wanted to survive this mess. They didn't seem to be very impressed with our explanation, but we nonetheless kept trying to persuade them: "Look, you're mature, reasonable people. The war is lost. If the Americans arrive here tomorrow and find you with rifles in your hands, they're going to shoot you all."

The men were unmoved by our arguments: "Nothing doing! We have our orders to hand stray prisoners over to the Gestapo in Wernigerode."

In April 1945, after three days of freedom, we were led away by four "respectable" old Germans, rifles at the ready, who handed us over to the Gestapo.

In Captivity Again

Still dressed in their floppy hats and leather coats, the Gestapo sent for a car and ordered us to get in. We were afraid they were going to spirit us away and shoot us. Instead, they drove us to Halle, where we got caught in a massive air raid. We sought cover in a mill built of brick. When we finally crawled out, we saw a variety of things floating down the Saale River, including something that made us very happy—a big picture of Adolf Hitler. "Take a look at that murderer over there," Ernst whispered to me. "Have no fear, though; his swimming days are numbered."

The Gestapo deposited us in a brand-new concentration camp near I. G. Farben's Leuna plant. The prisoners who had been collected there must have all been stragglers, because they weren't deployed in the forced-labor program. Two days later the SS guards made up some small cattle cars into a train. It left the camp on 12 or 13 April with us on board.

After a day's journey, punctuated by frequent air attacks, we were back in Halle. From there our odyssey took us all over Germany. During air raids the engineer would try to get the train to a wooded area as quickly as possible, out of sight of the fighter-bombers. Once, when we had stopped in some woodland we could see another train waiting on a sidetrack. Since our guards had cordoned off the area, the doors of the cattle cars were open. As I looked down the length of the train, I suddenly spotted a little fellow some distance away jumping out of one of the cars. I recognized him at once. It was Rolf Abrahamson, whom we had gotten to know when we were being trained as locksmiths, before he was deported to Riga in 1941. I called out and gestured to him. He climbed into our car and stayed with us.

As usual, the SS didn't give us any water. This time, however, we created such a ruckus while we were waiting for the train to start moving again that the engineer persuaded the SS to let us get some from his tender.

To appease our hunger we tried to cook grass and tree bark, but without much success. The more we cooked the grass the tougher it got.

The SS drove us back onto the train, and we continued our journey east. From that time on, the images in my memory become blurred. The only thing I remember is that I felt like killing anyone in the car who got too close to my bad knee. The pain was so intense that I bellowed like a bull. Finally, some of my fellow prisoners decided to make me a hammock out of a blanket, a couple of belts, and a pair of suspenders. They suspended it under the roof of the car. The hammock allowed me to avoid coming into physical contact with other people.

Liberation

I opened my eyes and saw Ernst sitting next to me on my bed.

"Where are we?" I asked.

"We're fine. The Russians have been in the area for two days now."

Ernst filled me in on what had happened during the last few days, while I was unconscious. The train had taken us to Theresienstadt, where the prisoners who had survived the trip tumbled out of the cars after the doors had been opened. Almost no one was able to stand, so they crawled on all fours to the barracks like monkeys. Nevertheless, my fellow prisoners managed to drag me along with them. I was unconscious and had a high fever. A few days later the Russians liberated Theresienstadt. But even after they arrived and had supplied the prisoners with the bare necessities, people were still dying by the hundreds.

I was close to death myself and probably wouldn't have survived longer than a week. If the Russians hadn't arrived, there wouldn't have been a Hans Frankenthal to write about.

There was a shortage of everything in Theresienstadt, especially drugs. A woman doctor, a major in the Soviet army, looked after us as best she could until the British and Americans showed up. The two Western Allies arrived with everything imaginable, from soup to nuts. But they ended up serving us a diet that consisted mostly of barley soup, which we called calves' teeth soup; the individual pellets were as large as a person's fingernails. The reason they decided to limit our diet was that our stomachs had to get used to real food again. In addition to the barley soup, though, they gave us as much bread as we wanted. So after a while there were pieces of bread everywhere—on top of bunks, under bunks, in the rafters—in every corner of the barracks. We tried to save every crumb we could.

When the people who were looking after us found out what we were doing, they were flabbergasted. They asked us why we were saving bread, since it would only become hard and dry. All we could do was stare at them. How could we make them understand that we were afraid we might not have anything to eat tomorrow? To us this seemed to be a perfectly normal way of looking at the world.

They subsequently collected all the bread we had saved and served us bread soup for the next few days. After that we went back to our diet of calves' teeth soup.

The daily mortality rate in the camp was extremely high. It took quite some time to contain the epidemic of typhus and dysentery. The sick were isolated in a special block. But the latrines were so small that the authorities ordered the construction of a series of corduroy roads in the Appellplatz.[24] The Nazis were then assigned the task of emptying these makeshift toilets every day.

It was a warm spring, and Ernst often carried me outside into the fresh air. There I repeatedly observed a little boy—he might have been six or seven years old—who had made it his responsibility to goad the Nazis into removing the raw sewage: "You killed my parents!" He hammered away at them as if they were pieces of brittle iron.

One beautiful spring day Ernst and I were sitting at the edge of a well in the middle of a square enjoying the sun. All of a sudden a woman made a beeline in our direction, came to a halt in front of us, and waited expectantly. It took a moment before we recognized her— it was Aunt Selma, our father's sister and the mother of Karl and Emil, the boys whom we had written from Monowitz.

Aunt Selma had been searching for us for several days. From her sons she had learned that we might still be alive. She told us how difficult it had been to find us among the seven to eight thousand people in the camp. We then shared important pieces of news with one another. Aunt Selma had had the courage to fend for herself in the hell of Theresienstadt. She had secured a tiny plot of land inside the huge ghetto, where she grew her own vegetables and managed to escape starvation. She had even seen Anna Stern, my father's elderly aunt, in the ghetto and was able to tell us the exact day on which Anna had died.

When Aunt Selma asked if there was something special I wanted, I told her I would very much like to have some milk. A little while later she returned with a big pitcher. We were extremely happy to have met a member of the family again and hoped to see more friends and relatives when we got back to Schmallenberg. We had no idea how many people had been murdered. . . .

It was during the next few weeks that various commissions began to organize the repatriation and emigration of displaced persons.

❁

Part II

The Return Trip

I was looking out the window of the bus and watching the Polish countryside drift by. The young people with whom I had spent the last few days in Auschwitz were seated around me and were chatting with one another.

This wasn't the first time I had visited the place I had sworn I would never set foot in again. However, it had taken over forty years before I took my first trip back and began to speak publicly about my life.

After liberation Ernst and I returned to the town of our childhood, Schmallenberg. We had complied with our father's wish. Even now I can hear the words he spoke to us on the loading platform at Auschwitz: "I won't survive this; I'm too old. If the two of you do, go back to Schmallenberg."

For many, many years afterward I cursed those words.

Arrival in Schmallenberg

In July 1945 a bus owned by the Rosenkranz Company, located in Witten, picked us up at Theresienstadt and drove us to Dortmund. We were to be taken to a hospital there for medical treatment. But Ernst and I refused to go, insisting that "all we need is a ticket to Schmallenberg."

Our persistence paid off. A short time later we boarded a train at the Dortmund railroad station that was headed for Hagen. We changed trains in Hagen and again in Schwerte and Altenhundem. We had our first encounter with a resident of Schmallenberg—Toni Störmann— at the railroad station in Altenhundem. Known as Demmen, Toni had been a foreman at the Jewish-owned firm of Artur Stern. He wasn't a Nazi.

First, I asked him what the latest news in Schmallenberg was. "My God, we were shelled for three days," he complained, "and a lot of houses were destroyed." Well, so they really did suffer a lot, I thought. I then asked if our parents' home had been destroyed as well. Toni replied that it hadn't. After we said good-bye to each other, I turned to him one last time: "You know what, Toni, as far as I'm concerned the whole town can burn to the ground."

For the last few kilometers the train traveled through a region in which we knew every village, farm, and footbridge.

The distance from the Schmallenberg railroad station to our parents' house on Obringhauserstraße was only a few meters. A private road connected the embankment to the piece of land where we used to take livestock for loading. We slowly walked down the road dressed in civilian trousers but still wearing our striped prisoner's coats. I stopped my brother in front of the steps to the front door of our home and asked him to take off his coat to make sure no lice got into the house. This was the first time in six years that we had set foot in our parents' home.

I hadn't shed a single tear during the past few years, but now I cried uncontrollably. It took me several hours to regain my composure.

First Encounters

My "half-Aryan" cousins Karl and Emil, Aunt Selma's sons, were living in the house at the time. Karl had returned from the Hagen-Haspe forced-labor camp. Emil had remained in hiding in Nesselbach near Altastenberg until liberation. They had received our letter from Monowitz before Karl's arrest and Emil's escape. They told us that they had gone to see Daniel Marburger, showed him the letter, and asked for the watch my father had entrusted to him. "I'll give the watch to the boys when they return," Marburger replied. "We can get the bread without it," he had told them before they went together to see Frau König. She wrapped up three loaves of bread and sent them directly to Jan Krupka. When I was in Auschwitz I didn't realize the number of lives I was putting at risk. If someone had discovered the letter, at least ten people would have been threatened with exposure, including my cousins, my brother, Jan Krupka, Daniel Marburger, and Frau König.

Ernst and I moved into the smallest room in the house. Dr. Deilmann, our father's former tax adviser, lent us a bed. But it took quite
some time before I could actually sleep in it.

I was unable to walk because of the pain in my knee. So I spent
the first few weeks lying on the sofa in the living room during the day,
eating and drinking a lot—today you might say I was on a permanent high—and receiving the visitors who came over to welcome us
back. Our neighbor, Theresia Rautekuss, had seen us return and went
around the neighborhood to announce the news. "The Frankenthal
boys are back!" The doorbell rang a lot. Without exception, the visitors were people who had stuck by us during the Nazi period. They
supplied us with food and clothing. In fact, a farmer from the neighboring village even sent us half a pig. In those days I didn't observe the
Jewish dietary laws; I didn't think I would ever believe in God again.
Frau König brought us a cake as well as the items our parents had
given her for safekeeping after Kristallnacht. My parents hadn't kept
an inventory of their belongings, but the Königs had made a list of all
the living room furnishings—every piece of furniture, every spoon, every cup, and every plate. They now returned the things to Ernst and
me. We were very happy that we had been able to count on them.

Among the first visitors to our house was the town's British military governor, who happened to be Jewish. He stood at the front door
with a large parcel under his arm. No sooner had he sat down than I
lit into him. Why hadn't the British allowed us to enter Palestine?
Why hadn't they bombed the railway lines and the crematoria at
Auschwitz? I myself could attest to the fact that secret messages had
been smuggled out of the camp with detailed maps of the facilities.
Moreover, we had learned that the information had reached London.
He refused to believe me. "If that had been the case, the government
or the military would definitely have done something."

Although we disagreed, I did give him something to think about.
During the next few days he made some inquiries and even learned
about a BBC broadcast that had reported on what had been going on
at Birkenau. When he visited me the next time, he confirmed what I
had told him. We spent a long time discussing the possible reasons for
the Allies' reluctance to bomb Auschwitz. I easily refuted his argument that bombing the gas chambers and crematoria would've killed
people too. I pointed out to him that the Sonderkommandos, the

special units of workers who cleared the bodies from the gas chambers and worked in the crematoria burning the corpses of the victims, were "switched" every four to six weeks, that is, they themselves were gassed and cremated. I sharply reproached the military governor—nonetheless, it was impossible to change the past.

Except for the military governor's visit, there was no official response to our return. We did receive a special temporary identification card, but it really didn't mean very much. Otherwise the town didn't give us so much as a thought. Dameries, the anti-Nazi mayor installed by the British, was obviously uninterested in our story or us.

We found it hard to talk to people unless we were absolutely certain that they had been on our side during the war. When my cousin drove me through town in his car and suggested from time to time that we stop, my only reply was: "I really have no desire to see anybody."

Even in the case of the townspeople whom we were now getting to know, there was one thing we still couldn't understand. None of them ever asked us what had happened to our parents or the other Jews who had lived in Schmallenberg.

Deeply disappointed, we tried to shake people up at first. We commissioned a sculptor who lived a few houses down from us to place the following inscription on a gravestone that we had put up in the center of town: "This is where the synagogue of Schmallenberg's Jewish community stood. It was pillaged and destroyed by the Nazis on 10 November 1938."

There was no response and no reaction from the town's inhabitants or the municipal authorities—nothing.

Aunt Hedwig

Of the fifty-one Jewish residents of Schmallenberg, only seven returned after the war. They included Ernst and me, Aunt Selma and her sons Karl and Emil, Helene Meyer, née Funke, and Hedwig Goldschmidt.

Helene—Lene for short—the wife of Uncle Ernst in Duisburg, my mother's brother, and Hedwig, Julius Goldschmidt's wife, had returned from the Riga ghetto. As usual, the town was oblivious to their existence. Lene and Hedwig moved into three rooms made available to them by the current owner of the Funkes' "Aryanized" house.

Unlike others who had returned from the camps, Hedwig was more or less healthy. But she said little if anything about the last few years.

Her husband, Julius Goldschmidt, had been released from Sachsenhausen in early 1939 because the Nazis needed his signature in order to "Aryanize" his property. On signing the sales contract, he committed himself to leave Germany within twenty-four hours. The authorities immediately issued passports to members of his family. The passports were stamped with a "J" and the following notation: "For a single crossing of the borders of Germany."

The Goldschmidts' eldest son, Leo, fled after the Nazis had arrested his father Julius and members of the National Labor Service (Reichsarbeitsdienst) had destroyed his father's shop.[1] Before he went to see his Uncle Alfred Funke in Duisburg to help speed up the process of emigrating to America, Leo had hid in the woods.

The rest of the family went their separate ways after Julius's release. Like Leo, Aunt Hedwig and her two daughters, Ruth and Lore, went to Duisburg to make preparations for emigrating. Julius, who had to leave Germany immediately, fled with his youngest son Heinz to Belgium by way of Holland, where they later fell into the hands of the Nazis. They were both murdered in Auschwitz.

Aunt Hedwig and her two daughters never managed to emigrate. They were deported to Riga in the first transport from Duisburg. Hedwig and my Aunt Lene met each other by chance in the Riga ghetto. Many years later Lene told Hedwig's son Leo in America that she, Lene, was able to protect his family for a time by working as a seamstress. First, she worked for the wife of the commandant of the ghetto and later for the commandant himself and for the SS. However, only Hedwig and Lene survived. Hedwig's daughters Ruth and Lore and her brother Alfred as well as Lene's husband Ernst were murdered in Stutthof.[2]

After Hedwig returned to Schmallenberg her son Leo visited her. He was an American soldier at the time and was stationed in Heidelberg. He advised his mother to rest and take care of herself while he obtained the necessary papers in America and made arrangements to bring her to the United States. But before Leo could complete the formalities, Hedwig died.

One day Aunt Lene called us on the telephone and begged us to come over immediately. Aunt Hedwig had gone to bed, she told us, and said she wanted to die. We went to see her and kept telling her that she was perfectly healthy. Even the doctors couldn't find anything wrong with her. But nothing helped. She was a psychological wreck and had lost the desire to live. She died a few days later. We buried her in the Jewish cemetery in Schmallenberg. In 1936 the Jewish community had purchased land to expand the cemetery. Who could have imagined then that practically all the Jews of Schmallenberg would end up being buried in a place called Auschwitz?

We composed the following inscription for Aunt Hedwig's headstone: "Having survived three and a half years of suffering in a concentration camp, you died of heartache because your husband Julius Goldschmidt, your son Heinz Goldschmidt, and your daughters Ruth and Lore Goldschmidt were caught in the Nazis' clutches, never to return."

Stumbling Blocks

I needed a lot of time to recuperate. The wounds from the inflammation on my legs were still open when I returned to Schmallenberg. With a few pills supplied to me by the British, however, the wounds soon began to heal—leaving me with deep scars.

My knee was a bigger problem. As in the case of my legs, I asked a British doctor to examine my knee at the high school in Schmallenberg. I was putting my clothes back on behind a curtain after the examination when I accidentally overheard the doctor discussing my condition with his assistant, Luzie Hatzfeld. Luzie was the daughter of my mother's seamstress. "There's nothing more we can do for him; he's going to die."

"Luzie," I yelled, "give my best regards to your doctor and tell him if I survived Auschwitz, I'll survive this too."

But I misjudged the severity of my illness. It took months for me to get back on my feet. In spite of the treatment I received, the pain in my knee didn't really go away. Luckily I had no idea what else was in store for me.

Soon after the war, we began receiving CARE packages on a weekly basis. Among other things, they contained two cartons of cigarettes. We soon got into the habit of smoking and began trading the farmers some of our cigarettes for food. Together with the little distillery we had in our basement, we were able to augment our other income.

In 1946 I heard through the grapevine that Alfred Funke's car was still in Schmallenberg, parked at the home of Peter Drenk, a fanatical Nazi. I headed straight for Drenk's house, opened the garage door without asking for permission, and found the vehicle—a specially made-to-order four-cylinder Ford with a fitted trunk where Funke used to put the sample case he took with him when he traveled from place to place to solicit business orders.

When Drenk saw me on his property, he shot out of his house in a rage.

"What are you doing here?"

"I want the car."

"No way! Get the hell out of here!"

I went to see an acquaintance of mine in the police department and asked him to help me.

"I'm sorry, Hans, it's not that easy. We can't just go there and pick up the car, even if it was acquired illegally. As soon as we open the garage door, we could be charged with trespassing. You'll have to go to the military government authorities."

I took my acquaintance's advice and spoke with some people in the military government. They told me to come back in a few hours, after they had had a chance to discuss the matter with the next-higher authority. When I returned, they gave me a letter from the military governor of the town ordering Drenk to surrender the car.

I took a few friends along to help me give the car a push. When I rang the bell at Drenk's house, he was just as nasty as he had been earlier. Since I didn't want to hassle with him, I went directly to the police again. This time they helped me. After reading the letter from the military governor, they sent two police officers to go with me to Drenk's place. Before Drenk finally surrendered the vehicle, they had to threaten him with arrest.

I used the Ford to begin dealing in livestock. I drove around the villages buying small domestic animals from the farmers and slaughtering them illegally.

As soon as I got most of my strength back I decided to rebuild my father's business. But when I applied for a business license, I was told that since I wasn't twenty-one, that is, hadn't come of age yet, I needed to have a guardian. Angry, I snapped at the official, "I didn't have a guardian when I was in Auschwitz, and you're telling me that I have to have one now."

The municipal authorities refused to budge until our tax adviser, Dr. Deilmann, said he would act as my conservator; I would never have accepted a guardian.

After the trading license took effect, I was faced with the next set of problems: I was unable to obtain permission to carry on a business; I wasn't given contract notes, and so forth and so on. Although the government agency in Unna-Königsborn responsible for issuing the necessary permits—in Hitler's time it was called the Reichsnähr-stand—now went under a different name, the bureaucrats who manned it were the same people who had staffed it under the Nazis.[3] No one made any allowance for the fact that you were a Jew or had survived the Holocaust. On the contrary, if you mentioned your background they discriminated against you. Even though people didn't express their prejudices openly, we could sense them. Whenever people could put obstacles in our way, they did so. We soon came to realize how the inhabitants of the Catholic Sauerland really felt: Now that virtually all the Jews were dead and gone, others should be discouraged from ever coming back again.

After tedious negotiations I finally completed the necessary formalities to operate a business. Still, there were frequent confrontations between the cooperatives, the "Aryan" livestock dealer Robert Krämer, and myself. Whenever we encountered each other, things got nasty. The non-Jewish livestock dealers pushed their prices up so that the animals cost more than I could afford. Or they tried to set the farmers against me. "What, you mean you're doing business with Jews again?"

Nor did I always have an easy time with the farmers. For example, they would often tell us the following story. "You know that we always stood by you and your family. We sold your father our last cow, our very last cow." I heard the same story umpteen times a day until I couldn't stand it any more and finally shot back: "My God, we only had space for twenty cows in the stall and all of you claim to have sold us your last cow? You know we never had that much room!"

Denazification in Schmallenberg

During the denazification proceedings in Schmallenberg, we were called as witnesses for the prosecution and testified against several persons, including Robert Krämer, the livestock dealer. When the case of Max Stern's broken windows came before the tribunal, Krämer asked a friend of his, a farmer named Kewekordes, to testify for the defense. When asked what he knew about the incident, Kewekordes answered with breathtaking audacity: "I didn't see or hear anything with regard to the windows."

Yet after the incident had taken place, the windows in Max's shop no longer had any windowpanes. And to make sure that every resident of Schmallenberg could see what had happened, Max went out of his way to cover the windows with cardboard. So for several days the broken windows were the main topic of conversation in town. I found Kewekordes's statement such a barefaced lie that I couldn't restrain myself and began shouting: "Kewekordes, they're showing a movie in Schmallenberg right now called *Der Meineidbauer* (*The Farmer Who Perjured Himself*)—why don't you go see it!"

In this case the citizens of Schmallenberg were on my side.

Although Krämer had other skeletons in his closet—he had supplied straw to the SA men who had set fire to the synagogue during Kristallnacht—the tribunal decided there wasn't conclusive proof that he had been a Nazi.

Amtsinspektor Holthaus, who still had his old job, was also summoned to appear before the tribunal. Most of my testimony against him focused on the day he had showed up at my parents' house and blackmailed my mother and other Jewish women by threatening to have their husbands killed. Because he had joined the Nazi Party early and grown rich on the property of Jews—the houses of my Uncle Sally and Julius Frankenthal—the military government dismissed him from his post. But just six weeks after the Federal Republic of Germany had been established, Holthaus once again had his old job back, the second-highest civil service position in Schmallenberg. Former Nazis stuck very close together.

Holthaus wasn't the only person who continued to live his life largely undisturbed. Ortsgruppenleiter Hermann Gilsbach likewise got off nearly scot-free. Like Holthaus, he had been in my mother's living room on that night in 1938. On another occasion I had clashed with him directly. Once, when Jews were allowed to shop only at certain times of the day, I found that there was something I absolutely had to buy immediately. So even though the law forbade me to shop,

I went to the Königs' grocery store. Hermann Gilsbach could often be found drinking schnapps at the bar in the adjacent König Café. He saw me enter the café and then followed me into the grocery. Cursing loudly, he kicked me in the pants and threw me into the street.

Like other Ortsgruppenleiters, he was arrested by the British soon after Germany surrendered in 1945. But he quickly resurfaced in Schmallenberg. In 1946, as I was driving my Ford, I saw him walking down the street. I pressed on the accelerator and headed straight for him. . . . He managed to jump behind a tree just before I could run him over.

The following day, Dr. Deilmann called me to his office and told me that Gilsbach had lodged a complaint with him. He wanted to know from me what I had done the previous day.

"Me?" I asked innocently. "I can't remember what I did yesterday."

"You drove your car straight for Hermann Gilsbach, didn't you?"

"Yes, that's right, and if he had only stood still, you'd be burying him now."

I thought it was my perfect right to do what I had done. Most Nazis were never called to account. Like so many others, Ortsgruppenleiter Gilsbach adapted to the new circumstances. And the other residents of Schmallenberg simply swam with the tide.

People were totally indifferent to the former Nazis. It didn't matter to them who had done what in the past. Tigges, the carpenter, for instance, used to stand on the sidewalk on Sundays in his SA uniform during the Nazi period and carp at people going to church. After the war, however, when it was decided to renovate the parish church in Schmallenberg, it was Tigges who was given the job of doing the carpentry work.

As soon as I found out about this, I got on the phone and informed the priest about Tigges's past conduct. "Herr Frankenthal," I had to listen to him tell me, "you believe in God—you have to learn to forget."

People simply took no notice of our past or us. And when the Cold War began, things got even worse. Denazification was a farce.

Registering with the Police

The town's first response to our reappearance came in the form of a verbal request. We were asked to come to the courthouse to register as residents of the town of Schmallenberg. But Ernst and I informed the town courier, Heinrich Schmidt, that we didn't see why we had to register. After all, we had never changed our residence of record. A few days passed after Schmidt's unsuccessful mission. He then showed up again at our door and informed us that if we didn't appear at the courthouse, we wouldn't get any ration cards. So we let ourselves be talked into going.

When we arrived at the courthouse, however, the first thing we did was to sit down on the front steps and refuse to go any farther. A small crowd gathered, before town officials finally persuaded us to enter the building.

Seated at a desk in the registration section was Ferdinand Hüte-mann, one of the men who used to stamp our ration cards with a "J." I immediately protested. "I'm not going to answer any of your questions! I never again want to have anything to do with Nazis like you."

The officials had no alternative but to get someone else. In the end we sat across from a man named Rickert. He came from a small farm in Werpe. Ernst and I listened silently as he explained what the town wanted from us. When he was through, I began to speak. "Have you finished with your questions?"

"Yes."

"Do you wish to know anything else?"

"No, we're just waiting for your response."

"Here it is! Just find our birth certificates in your files and copy the answers off them. I don't have to register with the police in the town I was born in and where I lived for so many years."

The officials turned crimson and searched for the birth certificates that contained the required information so that they could copy it. When they asked us what our nationality was, I said: "Stop! Let's end this right now. The answer is 'stateless.' I don't want to have anything more to do with this country."

"Listen here, you can't do that. You were born in Schmallenberg, in Germany. You're a German citizen."

At that time I didn't know that after we had been deported in 1943 we had been stripped of our German citizenship.

While Rickert was neatly and tidily filling out his forms, I caught a glimpse of our birth certificates. I thought my eyes were deceiving me. The following handwritten note entered in 1938 by Hohmann, the registrar, was emblazoned on the document: "The father and legal guardian of the illegitimate child [entered on the accompanying birth certificate] declares that the child shall bear the added given name 'Israel.' The names of both the father and the child are listed opposite this note on the birth certificate." Signed: Hohmann.

Underneath was a note entered in 1948: "The above marginal note is herewith annulled by order of the State President of Westphalia per ¶ 134 of the regulations." Signed: Hohmann.

Confrontations

After I returned to Schmallenberg I became politically active. I joined the KPD, because Communists had saved my life and because they were the most sincere politically involved people I knew.[4] I had met a number of Communists in Auschwitz who sacrificed everything to save people's lives. Without them, no Jew would have survived Auschwitz.

While I was a member of the KPD in Schmallenberg, the CDU was founded.[5] "Come on," I said to Ernst, "let's go over and see what's happening at their meeting, what kind of people show up."

We were among the first to be seated in the assembly room and saw one Hitler Youth leader after another come in. Many of the foremost CDU people in Schmallenberg were former Nazi officials.

Nevertheless, I later joined the CDU, which naturally confounded a lot of people.

Whenever I'm asked why of all parties I joined the CDU, I have to admit that back then I thought I might be able to give the members something to think about. Time and again I tried to make them understand that the leadership of the CDU, from its highest echelons down to the state legislatures and the county governments, was filled with former Nazis. I cited Globke and Filbinger as examples. Globke was the state secretary in charge of Chancellor Adenauer's office. He had written a commentary on the Nuremberg Laws.[6] Yet the CDU people acted as if they knew nothing. "Racial laws? What racial laws?" I might as well have been talking to a wall.

When I mentioned the fact that just before the end of the war Filbinger had sentenced three or four soldiers to be shot, the CDU people had a quick comeback. "OK, we agree the Nazi period is a fact. But let bygones be bygones. These people didn't commit any crimes. They have a perfect right to keep their jobs."

When I brought up the subject of Auschwitz and the persecution of the Jews, their reactions became even more extreme. Everybody—and I mean everybody—claimed total ignorance. And yet I knew many people in Schmallenberg who had been Nazis.

Even among friends and people my own age the subject was taboo. As soon as I touched on it, they'd say: "Yeah, yeah, we know. But enough is enough. You've got to draw the line somewhere."

You have to give the Germans credit. They really pulled off quite a coup, keeping something of such horrific dimensions repressed and under wraps.

The last confrontation I had was with a policeman. I had driven my car to Wiedenbrück to buy a new livestock trailer. On my way back I thought I'd drop by the stock sale in Dortmund and pick up a head or two of cattle. I left the sale with my trailer fully loaded and a short time later a policeman pulled me over in Totenberg, outside Neheim-Hüsten. He asked me to show him my ID, which I did. After walking around my trailer, he came over to speak to me. "Don't you know that you're not allowed to haul anything if you just have a trip permit? A trip permit just lets you tow the trailer from the place you purchased it."

"I know that, but as luck would have it, I bought two animals on the spur of the moment and put them in there anyway."

The policeman—a broad-shouldered hulk of a man over six feet tall—refused to discuss the matter. He just became more truculent and vociferous. I was very sensitive to German men in uniform and easily provoked, so I paid him back in kind. "You don't like the shape of my nose, do you? I guess you've figured out what my background is? Are you taking it out on me because you lost the war? You Nazi!"

The altercation grew increasingly heated. The policeman became so furious that I grabbed the jack handle from the back of my car and threatened him with it. "If you don't hightail it out of here right now, I'll bring this thing down on your head. At least I'll have the satisfaction of knowing I killed a Nazi."

He was stunned. I got back into my car and sped away.

Three or four weeks later Wilfried Bracht, a policeman who was a friend of mine, rang my doorbell. Since we still didn't have a police station in Schmallenberg, all police business was conducted on a person-to-person basis. "Tell me what you did," he asked. I told him I hadn't done anything. "You threatened to kill one of my fellow officers and called him a Nazi." "I did call him a Nazi—that's true. Whether I intended to kill him, I can't say for sure, but if he hadn't left, I might've."

The police took the matter to court, and a short time later I received a summons to appear before the district court in Arnsberg—the Federal Republic of Germany versus Hans Frankenthal. After the indictment was read, the judge asked me, "Herr Frankenthal, are the charges true?"

"Yes they are, Your Honor."

"And what do you have to say in your defense?"

"When I'm confronted with a big man like that, a colossus, all I see is the men who murdered my parents. I'm firmly convinced that he knew I was a Jew. Why don't you ask him what unit he served in during the war? Was he in the Waffen SS or the Wehrmacht?"

"Herr Frankenthal, that's beside the point."

"But couldn't you just do me the favor, Your Honor?"

The judge asked the policeman if he wished to answer the question. When the policeman said no, I cried out, "That's proof enough for me that he was in the SS."

The judge retired to his chambers.

It took a while for him to announce his verdict. He then noted the statute I had violated and added the following statement: "Herr Frankenthal, we cannot let you off scot-free. However, we have taken your background and agitated state of mind into consideration. Do you agree to pay the fine of three hundred deutsche marks?"

Needless to say, I agreed.

My ability to sense former Nazis had led to a number of similar clashes before the incident described above. After this last confrontation, however, I was forced to think seriously about what I should do next. Should I forget that horrible period in my life and act as if nothing had happened?

In the end I became convinced that it would be better to keep my mouth shut, since nobody believed me anyway and all I kept doing was landing in trouble. So for quite some time I avoided the temptation to talk about the subject.

Starting a Family

I met my future wife, Annie Labe, in 1947 when she was working as a kitchen aid at the Habbel Inn. We hit it off immediately and soon began discussing wedding plans. There was one problem, however. I was Jewish. It was customary in the Sauerland for a fiancé to introduce himself to his future in-laws. My wife had already forewarned these good Christian folk that I wasn't a Christian. "What is he, then?" they asked.

"He's a Jew."

"Oh my God."

Although Annie managed to get their approval, my in-laws constantly brought the subject up. During one of our visits they finally told us what bothered them most. "What about the children? How are you going to raise them?"

My wife and I had already resolved that we would let our children decide for themselves later which religion they wished to practice. For the time being, my in-laws said, they agreed with our decision.

Annie and I married in September 1948. In our wedding photo you can clearly see my swollen cheek. I hadn't yet taken care of my hollowed-out molars, even though parts of the crowns had gradually broken off. I suffered from one abscess in the jaw after another. Needless to say, I wasn't fond of dentists. But since nothing helped anymore, I forced myself to go see one. I summoned up my courage and made an appointment with Dr. Alwin Balzer, who had been my father's dentist. Balzer had been a first lieutenant in World War I and still behaved like an army officer, even toward his patients.

"Open your mouth wide!" he said as if he were issuing an order.

After he finished examining my damaged mouth, he asked: "What happened to you?"

I gave him a brief explanation. Although he was clearly outraged, I didn't let up. "I bet you'll benefit as a result of this."

"How's that?"

"You know, they were conducting experiments in Auschwitz."

"Look, there are so many reports being published every day about new techniques in the field of dentistry. I'm sure no one wants to read about dental research in Auschwitz."

First, he pulled the lower molars on the right side of my mouth and two days later the upper pair on the same side. Then he pulled the lower molars on the left side, and so forth and so on, until he had removed them all.

The following night I woke up with my mouth full of blood. "What's wrong?" my wife asked, half asleep.

"I don't know. Wait a minute, I'll go rinse my mouth out."

After I had finished, I felt and then saw a small stream of blood coming from a tooth socket. I called Dr. Balzer. "I have postoperative bleeding."

"You don't say so?" he replied in his military manner.

"Yes I do."

"Take a terrycloth towel, bite on it hard, and the bleeding will stop."

I bit on the towel for two hours but the bleeding continued. I had no alternative but to drive to his office in the middle of the night. Dr. Balzer received me wearing a white coat over his pajamas. It took a little while until we managed to stop the bleeding.

Over the next several weeks Dr. Balzer replaced the missing teeth. I hadn't even reached the age of thirty and I already had false teeth.

The first years of my marriage were extremely happy. Annie was always ready to lend a hand and helped me greatly in carrying on the livestock business. We worked a lot together. We hardly ever talked about Auschwitz, though. She was well aware that my family, like almost all the Jews in Schmallenberg, had been murdered and that my brother and I had been in Monowitz. But I never talked with her about the details. Whenever she asked me about my experiences, I tried to duck the question.

Nevertheless, Annie shared some of the aftereffects of those horrific years. Not only was I a very restless sleeper, I talked in my sleep as well. Whenever I was pursued by my dreams, I would cry out and scream at night. Certain images from Monowitz kept recurring. I dreamed about the beatings at the construction site . . . and being forced to watch people being flogged in the Appellplatz . . . about Max Stern, whom we had dragged back to the camp with us. I saw *Muselmänner* and suddenly recognized myself among them, a human shadow ready to collapse . . . on the verge of death. In my dreams I was also tormented by the unspeakably horrible events during the three days and nights in the cattle car as we were transported from Dortmund to Auschwitz. And sometimes I would wake up just before freezing to death in the open tender—dripping with perspiration and overcome by panic.

The Children of the Survivors

Adelheid, our eldest daughter, was born in 1950. Our son, Hans Dieter, was born in 1952 and our youngest child, Anita, in 1954. When Anita was born the priest thundered from the pulpit that there were children being born in Schmallenberg who weren't being baptized. Little heathens!

People broke the news of the priest's words to me gently; Annie gave me somewhat more detail. In any case, this was the event that triggered some changes in our life. Annie and her parents began to pressure me. "You see! Now we're in for it. We've got to do something. Adelheid is going to start school soon. When she's asked what her religion is, what is she supposed to say?"

The three of them kept on and on at me until I finally gave in. "Do what you will!" I said.

They got in touch with the priest. It was decided that the three children would be baptized in the near future, all at the same time. I told Annie and her parents I had just one favor to ask of them. "Please don't do it publicly, in the church. You can do it in the sacristy if you like. But I just don't want to see a crowd in front of the church. I won't be going with you anyway—I'll be on the road that day—but I just don't want to have all the residents of Schmallenberg standing there watching."

My children were baptized in due course. That didn't solve our problems, though. Later, as Adelheid was about to take her First Communion and she and her mother entered the nave of the church, some people sitting in the pews muttered. "What's that Jew girl doing here in her little white dress, taking Communion?"

My daughter didn't tell me about the incident until the late 1980s. And my wife kept silent about it, too. She knew that if I had been there, I would've turned right around and walked out of the church.

I deeply regret now that I didn't raise my children as Jews, but in those days I left their upbringing largely to my wife. My relations with my children were never easy. I had so much work to do that I hardly ever saw them. I seldom got a chance to play with them or hold them in my arms. On the other hand, when it came to money and presents, I was extremely generous. They always got whatever their hearts desired. A few years ago, when I complained about my children to our neighbor, Theresia Rautekuss, she reproached me. "Why are you complaining? It's your fault. When our kids went to the schuetzenfest, we gave them ten marks. Your kids got fifty."[7]

I wasn't able to talk with my children about my past. When they asked me about the tattoo on my arm, I explained that it was an important telephone number that I dare not forget. Many other people asked me the same question. In the beginning I tried to tell them the truth. But since they invariably reacted with disbelief or became defensive, I replied with the same little white lie that I told my children. Should I have let my children know that their grandparents had been murdered at Auschwitz? If I had, they might've talked about it on the school playground and been forced to listen to their classmates call their father a liar. I wanted to spare them the embarrassment.

At the same time, however, I tried to acquaint them with the facts, using a different approach. When they came home after playing and said they were hungry, I would tell them: "You're not hungry. *We* were hungry. You just have an appetite for something; you're not hungry."

I assumed that Annie had spoken with the children and explained to them why I sometimes acted so strange. I could never make myself talk to my children directly or in any detail about my past.

Many survivors found it difficult to discuss their experiences. They wanted to forget the horror and simply couldn't speak about it—and the Germans, of course, never asked the survivors any questions.

Even among ourselves we avoided discussing the subject. After 1945 there were still a few Jews who sold livestock to the slaughterhouses. Whenever we ran into somebody we knew was Jewish, we would ask him, perhaps just in passing: "Where did you survive the war?" If we got an answer at all, it was usually curt—"in the camp" or "in the ghetto"—and that was it. We had no desire to make an issue of the matter—and the Germans didn't want to hear about it anyway.

I ran into Max Rosenstein by chance in 1947 at the slaughterhouse in Dortmund. He had endured everything along with us. He never mentioned his child, who had been killed in Auschwitz, or anything else related to his time in the camp. Before being deported to Auschwitz, Max had five children. We were told that his wife had been pregnant with his sixth. He returned from the camp in fairly good health, remarried, and had three children with his new wife. He gave them the names of his murdered children.

Maybe psychiatrists should have advised the survivors of the camps not to have children after liberation in 1945, because we were never able to give them enough love.

Ernst

My brother Ernst didn't care to discuss the period before 1945 either. He said he no longer had any memory of that time. I almost believed him, until I accidentally found out nearly forty years later that he could still recall the names of our friends who had been hanged three days before the evacuation of the camp.

After we returned to Schmallenberg, Ernst found out that Margot Menzel, the love of his youth from Bochum, had also survived the war. They were married in 1946 and moved into the upstairs section of my parents' house. Annie and I lived downstairs. In the beginning Ernst helped me run the livestock business. But after he had completed his practical training at the Stratemann Opel dealership in Dortmund— formerly a Jewish-owned firm—he planned to buy or lease a service station. He found a suitable location along the Möhne River, but his doctor told him that operating a gas station was the worst possible thing he could do for his health. The underlying cause of the jaundice he had developed in Monowitz hadn't been effectively treated. Because of his damaged liver and gallbladder, Ernst already had to watch his diet very carefully. Now on top of that, his doctor warned him that inhaling gasoline fumes could lead to liver failure.

After Ernst and Margot's daughter Ruth was born, Margot's uncle, Siegfried Goldenberg, asked the family to move to Münster. Siegfried and his wife had survived the Riga ghetto but had lost all their children. Now they wanted to be close to young children again. So in 1948 my brother and his family moved to Münster, where he and Siegfried opened a fish market.

A second child, their son Uriel, was born in Münster. He was just two years old when his mother died of cancer in her mid-fifties. Since

Margot was still young we always assumed that her premature death was a result of the suffering she had endured.

After a few years Ernst was forced for reasons of health to give up his job at the fish market. He married a second time and took over a magazine stand where he also sold lottery tickets. After he died on 11 June 1993, his son Uriel carried on the business.

The Knee Operation

In the early 1950s the pain in my knee became more severe. Since the treatment I had received in Schmallenberg hadn't corrected the condition, my physician referred me to Dr. Eckert, a specialist in charge of a clinic in Bigge.

After examining my X rays, Dr. Eckert called me in to his office and urged me to undergo surgery. He suspected I was suffering from tuberculous osteitis. I agreed to have the surgery and stayed in Bigge while preparations were made for the operation.

As I was recovering from the anesthesia, I noticed that my leg was in a cast all the way up to my pelvis. The doctors told me that what I had was in fact tuberculous osteitis and that they had had to remove the knee joint. No matter what the outcome of the operation, I would have a stiff leg.

"But first you have to get your health back. And at the moment there's only thing we can do—hope and pray," they said.

"Hope and pray," I snapped. "You mean to tell me that hoping and praying can make you healthy?"

In further discussions a doctor mentioned an antibiotic that might help but that was not yet available in Germany. When I asked him for more information, he told me it came from America and was called streptomycin. I immediately asked for access to a telephone and called Siegfried Heimberg in Dortmund. He had returned with us to Germany from Theresienstadt. When I explained my situation to him, he asked for the exact name of the drug and the total dose required. It was quite a lot—a hundred injections—but he reassured me: "Don't worry. I'll take care of everything."

Three days later the amount required for the standard treatment regimen appeared in Bigge. The Joint had supplied the drug.[8]

After a lengthy period of drug treatment during which I was given one injection a day, I recovered and felt more or less healthy. However, over the next few years I had to have several more operations. My leg has remained stiff ever since.

"Reparations"

At some point it became clear that at least I wouldn't die as a result of having been a prisoner in the camps. It was my expectation that the pensions granted to survivors—as reparations, or *Wiedergutmachung,* literally a "making good for"—would be sufficient to ensure that they wouldn't have to seek employment again. Incidentally, I never liked the term *Wiedergutmachung* because I felt that nothing could make up for the suffering we had endured. In any case, my expectations weren't fulfilled. To the contrary . . .

After the initial reparations settlement was approved in the Bundestag in the early 1950s, we sought Dr. Deilmann's assistance. In 1935 the tax authorities had conducted an audit of the Frankenthal brothers' business. This made it easier to document the losses the firm had incurred as a result of the decrease in sales after 1933 and facilitated the ultimate shutdown of the business. We calculated the loss in sales at around 350,000 marks. So we petitioned the West German government to compensate us for that amount.

A senior civil servant named Radtke asked me to come to the reparations office in Arnsberg. He informed me that, on the strength of my *Erbschein* (certificate of inheritance), I had a valid claim to reimbursement of all material assets.[9] However, I did not have a legitimate claim with regard to my father's business because in 1938 I was just twelve years old and my brother was only fourteen, that is, we didn't qualify as the legal owners of the business. "Therefore you are not entitled to claim reparations."

I was nearly speechless. Here we were, the children of murder victims, and yet we had no right to file a claim. On top of that, we were obliged to hear this from a former member of the SPD who had even spent a few weeks in a Nazi jail.[10] And now we had to haggle with him over every penny.

We received no compensation for our father's business, just a one-time payment of 5,000 DM because we had been "prevented from learning a trade." An amendment to the law increased the size of the payment by an additional 5,000 DM. All told, we received 10,000 DM as reparations for slave labor, deportation, our lost youth, imprisonment in a concentration camp, the loss of all our relatives, lifelong physical and psychological problems . . .

It wasn't until the early 1960s that we officially got our parents' house back. In 1945 the municipal authorities had told us that although we could consider ourselves the owners, they could not yet transfer title to us. We first had to pay the town 1,300 DM as compensation for the 13,000 reichsmarks that my father had presumably received after the forced "sale" of his assets in the wake of Kristallnacht. Incidentally, the Nazis had deducted 8,000 RM from that amount to help pay the so-called *Judenbuße,* or "Jews' fine," that had been imposed on the Jewish community under the pretext of reparation for having caused the pogrom. At any rate, not only did the Schmallenberg municipal authorities not compensate us for a rundown house in need of renovation or for the lost rental income—they made *us* pay *them.*

Trying to obtain compensation was a devastating experience. There were hundreds of special regulations. And the formula used to compute claims invariably favored the government. You had to go through a huge bureaucratic labyrinth to obtain every penny. After arguing with reparations officials for years, I finally stopped getting upset and just gave up.

The Federal Republic of Germany never provided reasonable compensation for the financial losses we had incurred.

Nor was there much hope of claiming that we had a right to a full pension. My stiff knee, the deep scars on my lower legs, my ruined teeth didn't matter.

After my capacity to work and earn a living was evaluated, I received a disability rating of 40 percent and was granted a partial pension of 93.33 DM a month.

Ernst also wished to find out the extent to which his chronic liver condition had reduced his earning capacity. After a doctor examined him in Münster, he phoned me.

"Do you want to know what rating I received?"

"All right. Fifty, sixty percent?"

"Zero."

"Come again? Zero?"

"Yes, zero!"

I was outraged. So I tried to find out more about the doctor who had examined my brother. I inquired at the office of the Vereinigung der Verfolgten des Naziregimes (Association of Persons Persecuted by the Nazi Regime) and learned that he had been a member of the Nazi Party. This wasn't a good omen. We were often confronted with doctors who had either practiced medicine before 1945 or had been Nazis and still believed in the Nazi ideology. These were the men who were now responsible for rating us for disability pensions.

Being rated was bad enough, but the reaction of people in the street was even worse. They would come up to me and to other survivors and tell us we had nothing to complain about. After all, we had no more money worries. Why, you must be getting at least 10,000 DM a month in pension benefits, they would say. People actually said these things to me openly on the street. "Well, why don't you come home with me," I'd tell them, "and take a look at my financial records. But bring a hankie along; you're going to need it."

A Very Ordinary Citizen of Schmallenberg

To tell the truth, I was, beginning in the 1950s—how should I put it—very much the ordinary citizen. I was a member of practically every organization in Schmallenberg—except for those that were too closely associated with National Socialism. I was a welcome member of the rifle club, the men's chorus, and the bowling club. I was on friendly terms with most people in town—except for the ten individuals who I knew had played an important role in the Nazi Party. And I carefully avoided them. Otherwise I got together with my friends at club meetings or at the tavern to play cards. Once a year the whole bowling club would make an excursion during which we would have lots of fun together. The bowling club played a particularly important part in my life, and I spent a great deal of my leisure time there. Most of the members were tradesmen—locksmiths, plumbers, butchers, and so forth.

On the whole, I felt quite at home in Schmallenberg. Only occasionally did something happen to remind me that I was "different." In the 1960s I took part in the rifle club's competition. When I was just

one shot or two from winning the title of champion marksman, I
turned to the members of the board who were standing directly behind
me and asked: "Is it all right with you if I continue shooting?"
Everyone knew why I had asked the question. The board members
simply told me to keep on firing. The rifle club, they said, didn't have
a problem with those kinds of things.

I went on to win the title. A number of the residents of Schmallenberg shared my joy with me. But when we went for a lunchtime drink
after the match was over, a rumor started making the rounds that An-
ton Irmler, the gardener, had asked some of the members of the rifle
and bowling clubs whether they wanted to march in a parade through
town behind a Jew. No sooner did I learn what he had said than I went
to the members of the board and asked them what they thought about
the matter. Slightly tipsy, they replied: "That's a bunch of garbage!
Our decision is final!"

The rest of the year was uneventful until the subject came up again
at the next shooting match. A Mass was held for the rifle club—an
early Mass before the beginning of the new competitions. It was customary to have the reigning champion marksman and the new champion marksman, along with two of his officers, stand in front of the
high altar during the service. In the days preceding the Mass, word got
around in Schmallenberg that Father Ernst had said he didn't want to
have a Jew stand in front of the high altar. So I decided to turn the
tables on him. I said that I had no intention of opposing his wishes and
would invite my officers to the Störmann Hotel for a couple of beers
instead of attending the Mass. Naturally, most of the officers accepted
my invitation. The priest then did an about-face, but by that time I
had no desire to attend the Mass anyway. Instead I went with two of
my fellow club members to have a beer. I even refused to be part of the
honor guard that the priest passed by as he left the church after Mass.
In fact, I didn't get back into line until after he had disappeared into
his house.

When I wasn't reminded of recent history by unpleasant incidents
such as these, I tried to overlook the past. But of course whenever I
drove cattle and lost my footing because of my stiff leg and couldn't
stop myself from falling, you can imagine how much I cursed the time
I had spent in the camp.

When I was with friends I never brought up the past by myself.

Sometimes, however, in the course of an ordinary conversation at the bar in the Schmallenberg sports club, they would start boasting about their wartime experiences. This was quite common among Germans of my generation; even to this day the old guard can't break the habit. One was in Russia, another in France, another in Norway. . . .

Once, I kept silent until one of them turned to me and asked: "Say, Hans, where were you during the war?"

"Me? I was in Auschwitz."

They all looked at me: "Auschwitz? Where's that? In what country?"

"It used to be part of your lovely Germany. It was the site of an extermination factory where you Germans killed, shot, and gassed people!"

After a moment of silence all five of them bristled as if on command: "You're nuts! You're putting us on. That's absolutely unheard-of!"

"Listen," I replied, "you've lived in Schmallenberg a good long time. Eleven Jewish families used to live here and now there's just one. That means there are forty-four people in those families who are missing. Could you tell me where they are? I know the answer—but I'll give you a year, and if you can tell me where these people were living in 1945, I'll stand in the church square for twenty-four hours and yell 'I'm a liar' for everyone to hear."

Incensed, I stomped out of the tavern.

When we got together one or two days later, my friends wanted to know why I had gotten so upset.

"Because you refused to admit the crimes your fathers or you yourselves committed," I shouted at them.

"We didn't commit any crimes."

"Of course not, you were all angels. The Jews killed themselves."

Arguing with them was clearly an exercise in futility.

The Trial in Frankfurt

The Auschwitz trial began in Frankfurt on 20 December 1963. A few months earlier Ernst and I had been summoned to appear before the Fredeburg district court. We were informed that a trial was to take place to investigate what had happened at Auschwitz. Then we were questioned about what we remembered.

Later, I was summoned to appear as a witness in Frankfurt to testify about my period of imprisonment and the death marches.

After I finished giving my statement at the trial, the presiding judge had several questions for me. "Did you have much interaction with the SS? Would you mind walking past the rows of prisoners' boxes and taking a look at the defendants? You may take a piece of paper and a ballpoint pen with you. The defendants have numbers in front of them. If you recognize any of them, would you please write the numbers down?"

"May I ask one favor of you, Your Honor? Do I have to look into their faces?"

"If we ever hope to work through the past, you'll have to force yourself to do it."

With pen and paper in hand, I walked over to where the defendants were seated. After I had written the second or third number down, I suddenly saw a face that had long ago engraved itself in my mind. The man sitting in front of me was the same man who had kicked me and chased me from the infirmary when I tried to warn Ernst about the possibility of his being selected for extermination. The man's name was Neubert, an SS medical orderly. I stood stock-still and couldn't utter a word. I stared at him until he finally gave me a nod.

I continued walking down the row and recognized several other persons. After I told the court officials who I knew, where I knew them from, and what I knew about them, they asked me about the person I had stood in front of for such a long time. I then told them the story of my brother.

Reports about the trial appeared in the press. The residents of Schmallenberg were startled by headlines such as "Hans Frankenthal testifies at trial." Some even saw me on television. This was the era when the first TV sets appeared and people would drop into a bar to watch the evening news. In any case, citizens of Schmallenberg would suddenly stop me on the street and ask me to tell them about the proceedings.

"Why should I?" I would answer them. "So you can tell me the next day that you don't believe anything I told you? There's plenty of literature on the subject. Why don't you go get yourself some?"

Despite any negative experiences, we were truly grateful that the trial was taking place. After twenty years, people were talking openly about Auschwitz for the first time.

A Letter from Poland

Something else happened as a result of the trial in Frankfurt. In the early 1970s I discovered a letter from Poland in my mailbox. It was from Jan Krupka. I found out later that he had read my name in a Polish newspaper article about the Auschwitz trial. He subsequently wrote to the public prosecutor's office in Frankfurt to get my address. After the war Jan had become the mayor of Monowitz (Monowice). He described the devastating economic conditions in Poland and asked me for some help. We sent him a big parcel filled with everything we thought he might need.

A few weeks later a long thank-you letter from him arrived with some more requests. Without a moment's hesitation I invited him to visit Germany.

As a formality in accordance with the legal requirement, I hired him to work in the slaughterhouse. In this way I was able to bring him into the country and provide him with a few happy weeks. Since Jan was an enthusiastic angler, I obtained a license for him through a good friend of mine so that he could fish in the Lenne River. Every day he would come back with ten or twelve trout. And since he was an excellent cook, my fellow workers and I would sit down with him to enjoy them.

While he was staying with us, the Schmallenberg schuetzenfest took place. So I took Jan with me to the shooting matches, where I introduced him as the man who had smuggled our letter out of Monowitz. People's jaws dropped when they heard the story.

Eight weeks later, loaded down with a knapsack, suitcases, and parcels, Jan returned home a happier man.

At my suggestion, Ernst invited Jan to visit Münster the following year. I saw him two or three times at my brother's place. However, as the years passed we lost contact with each other.

The Children Grow Up

In 1975 I took over Josef Wilmes's butcher shop. He had died and his wife was looking for someone to lease it to until her son could take over the business. Together with my daughter Adelheid and my son Hans

Dieter, I built up a thriving party catering service. Its success was partly due to the fact that my fellow club members became our customers. My daughter, by the way, had earlier completed her apprenticeship as a shop assistant in a butcher shop owned by one of my customers in Olpe.

Adelheid was a very committed and capable salesperson. Hans Dieter would have preferred to go to college. However, when the question of his education came up, I prevailed and he ended up learning the butcher's trade. I wanted someone to succeed me in the business, and I made sure he apprenticed himself to a very demanding master butcher. Hans Dieter was good but not particularly happy in or committed to his trade.

Anita, my youngest child, had the best deal of all. I left her free to choose her occupation. Understandably, my two older children held this against me. And frankly, I have to admit that I did give preference to Anita. She always got whatever she wished for. At first she wanted to go to college, but after a year she lost interest in studying and gave everything up. Then she became a trainee at the Falke Company. She explained that she wanted to begin her training in a place where she truly enjoyed working. Later, however, she said the company wasn't the right place for her after all. Finally, she decided to study business management at Bielefeld University.

When the time came for her to leave for school, I got her a room through a friend of mine in Bielefeld and, after a gentle hint from her, a car as well.

"What kind do you want?"

"Oh, I'd be happy with a Citroën deux-chevaux."

It seemed as if I had hardly said good-bye to her as she took off in her new Citroën 2CV when I got a call from Anita an hour later somewhere on the way to Bielefeld. The roads were slippery and she had overturned the car between Meschede and Warstein. Luckily she wasn't hurt, but the car was a total loss. I picked her up, drove her to Bielefeld, had the 2CV towed away, and bought her a new car.

Anita completed her studies four or five years later and graduated with excellent grades. She immediately found a job.

As the years passed, my wife Annie and I grew apart from each other. I was never an especially faithful husband. In 1976—Anita was twenty-two years old—I had a steady girlfriend, and Annie gave me a choice: "Either you change your ways and give that woman up or I'll get a divorce. I'll give you a day to think it over."

"Wait—stop," I said. "I can give you the answer right now. I'm not going to change. Either we work out a compromise or it's over."

Shortly afterward a letter from a lawyer in Arnsberg arrived on my desk stating that my wife had filed for divorce.

Her lawyer presented her financial claims in divorce court. I chose not to contest any of them.

During the first few months I missed her very much. If she had come back, I would have reconciled with her. But she had had her fill of me. Our relationship was quite strained until our children married and our first grandchildren arrived. Since then, we have often been in touch with each other. If anybody needed anything, the telephone would ring and Annie would say: "Come on, why don't you help them out?"

From my grandchildren I learned that Annie was interested in politics and that she watched every documentary on TV that dealt with the Nazi period.

In the early 1980s I got estimates on how much it would cost to build a slaughterhouse in accordance with European Community guidelines. We had to move our butcher's business out of the residential area it was located in at the time. I was about to discuss the matter with my son when he looked at the numbers and said he didn't want to take the risk. The project would have required an investment of 2.5 million marks. At first I was miffed at him, but later I realized that he was right.

The upshot was that I stopped doing any slaughtering, expanded my livestock business a little, and sold part of my property. My bones were getting progressively worse, and I was beginning to think about retirement.

One winter's evening I spent some time with friends sitting in the ski lift in Schmallenberg (in the early 1970s I had invested some money in the project). I had had a little too much to drink. The last thing I remember after stepping off the lift was getting into my car to drive home and waking up the next morning in the hospital. I had fractured my thighbone, ruined my knee, and totaled my car.

The fracture turned out to be a long drawn-out affair. After I was discharged from the hospital, I began to wonder why I should keep struggling with the livestock business. So on 30 January 1981 I closed up shop and retired.

How It All Started Over Again

After I stopped working I became depressed. I was unhappy and felt isolated in Schmallenberg. I longed to be with other Jews and spent a great deal of time at the Jewish cemetery, unfairly reproaching the dead for having abandoned me.

I got into the habit of driving to Dortmund on Friday afternoons, renting a hotel room, and attending synagogue in the evenings and on Saturdays. At the beginning of the week I would head back to Schmallenberg. After returning from Auschwitz I doubted the existence of God. I would sometimes drive to the synagogue in Hagen in those days to pick up CARE packages, but I never stayed for services. For a long time I found it impossible to truly reconcile with God after what I had seen. Where was God in Auschwitz? Even now I can't find a rabbi anywhere who can give me a satisfactory answer.

However, as time passed I became a practicing Jew again. And those weekends in Dortmund became very important to me.

It was during this period of my life that I started having my old dreams again. Memories I could no longer repress came back to me. My psyche went on strike, as it were. I was tormented by the question why I had survived. I reproached Ernst and myself for having persevered while 6 million others had had to die. Had we been corrupted in the process? We had exploited every opportunity to get something to eat and had benefited from the support of Emil Meier and Ede Besch. I had shared every bite with my brother—but should we have also given food to another person? Then again, I asked myself, wouldn't all three of us have died as a result? Questions and reproaches thrust themselves upon me with such force that I found it impossible to escape them.

I had had these same kinds of feelings during the Auschwitz trial and after seeing the American TV series *Holocaust* in the late 1970s, which had a profound effect on me. I asked my family to watch the broadcast and then tried to explain to them how much more horrible the reality of the camp had been. But I still found it impossible to speak about my personal experiences. For a short time after the trial the citizens of Schmallenberg showed some interest in my story, but then everything was shrouded in silence again.

I became intensely interested in the subject of Auschwitz. I read every book, every newspaper and magazine article I could lay my hands on. It became an obsession.

I went to see my family doctor. I was having trouble sleeping and my legs were getting progressively worse. She referred me to a physician in Altenhundem. After examining me he wrote two reports—one on my psychological condition and another on my legs.

Since my health had clearly deteriorated, I sent the medical assessments to the regional social security office in Düsseldorf together with an application to upgrade my disability rating. A woman doctor there was responsible for reviewing claimants' medical evidence. In the meantime the skin on my legs began to turn purplish as a result of an inadequate blood supply. But without even examining me the doctor made a determination and upgraded my benefits by a mere 10 percent. When I received the letter from her informing me of her decision, I could hardly believe my eyes.

I called her up soon afterward. Our discussion quickly escalated and I threatened to become violent. She was so arrogant and inconsiderate that I decided to contact the Central Council of Jews in Germany. I found out that I wasn't the only survivor who had called to complain about her. When she went so far as to maintain in a written medical assessment that diabetes was a "hereditary Jewish disease," the Central Council finally intervened and saw to it that she was suspended from government service. Although she later returned to her former job, she was prohibited from writing any medical assessments in the future.

I was subsequently referred to Professor Kisker in Hanover. He had been asked to write a general assessment of my health. After giving me an exhaustive physical examination, he invited me into his office. Sitting behind his desk, he went through my medical file. "Herr Frankenthal," he said, "I hope you're not in a great hurry."

"What do you mean? I assume I'll be back home this afternoon. You have enough information on me now to expedite the review, don't you?"

Much to my surprise, he told me about a research project he was involved in that was studying the effects of the Holocaust on survivors. Since I was the first person he had ever met who had witnessed

Kristallnacht as a young boy, he asked me if I would tell him the story
of my life so that he could include it in his research.

I consented. But it was extremely difficult for me to do so. This was
the first time in forty years that I had talked in any detail about my
youth and the time in the camp.

After our session ended, I told Professor Kisker I would like to find
out something from him. "I've told you a lot about myself. Now I'd
like to ask you a question. Why is it that we survivors have to face all
this grief and all these problems only now, at this stage in our lives?
And how come we've been able to live with this whole business for
thirty years without having any problems?"

"You've managed in the same way the perpetrators have—by re-
pressing what you've been through. It has been pursuing you all along.
Now it's finally catching up with you."

I have long been preoccupied by the question whether the sixty-
and seventy-year-old perpetrators have to struggle with their memories in the same way as the survivors, who have been forced to go
through all their suffering and grief again in old age.

The Memorial Stone

As the only Jew in Schmallenberg in the early 1980s, I was invited by
the town council to the unveiling of a commemorative stone at the
place where the town's synagogue had stood.

Even though nobody had told me about the unveiling or sought my
advice in advance, I wrote to the town council to ask if it wouldn't be
appropriate on such an occasion to ask a rabbi to recite prayers for the
dead. Nobody voiced objections to my suggestion and the council
asked me to make the arrangements. I decided to invite Emil Davidovic, the chief rabbi of Westphalia and Lippe, to be present at the
ceremony.

As is the custom in a Catholic region such as the Sauerland, the unveiling took place on Sunday after High Mass. About two hundred
people gathered on Synagogenstraße. After the last speaker had finished, the stone was unveiled. I hadn't been told ahead of time what
the inscription read. So I couldn't believe my eyes when I saw it: "This
is where the synagogue of Schmallenberg's Jewish community stood
from 1857 to 1938." That was all!

In a speech delivered after the unveiling, Rabbi Davidovic was critical of the fact that the inscription made no reference to the destruction of the synagogue on Kristallnacht. He asked his audience to remember that many young people no longer knew what the year 1938 meant in the history of modern Germany. At the very least, he said, the inscription should have made reference to the perpetrators. Fittingly, the commemorative ceremony brought back some painful memories to the town of Schmallenberg.

The Long Silence of Amtsinspektor Holthaus

Whenever we spoke with the authorities about the return of Jewish homes and other assets to the heirs of the deceased proprietors, we would ask Franz Holthaus, the town's former Amtsinspektor, whether there were any documents pertaining to the period after 1933 in Schmallenberg. Time and again he said that there weren't.

Despite the fact that he had acquired Jewish property under the Nazis, Holthaus was highly respected by the citizens of Schmallenberg. He constantly said that he had made every effort to protect Jews. And at events such as the unveiling of the memorial stone at the site of the former synagogue, he always managed to force his way to the front of the crowd.

We almost believed him. Perhaps he had in fact done some things on behalf of the Jews of Schmallenberg. Then something happened that cast a new light on Holthaus's past.

In the mid-1980s Helga Tröster, a student in Fredeburg, began a research project on Jewish life in Schmallenberg. As part of her study she asked for and received from the town council a file containing reports relating to Jewish life in Schmallenberg from the late seventeenth century to 1933. She examined them and then continued her research in various other archives. But she approached the town council again later—she felt sure that there had to be documents relating to the period after 1933. Holthaus kept denying the existence of any such documents until Helga Tröster lost her patience and threatened to take legal action against the town. Suddenly additional documents seemed to appear out of nowhere. They were included in what was called "Special Files of the Schmallenberg Police Pertaining to Jewish Cultural Affairs/Jews" and covered the period 1933 to 1943.

Needless to say, I was quite interested in what she had found. So when Helga Tröster told me she was very sorry but that she hadn't been given permission to let me see the documents, I went straight to Amtsinspektor Weber. "Reinhold," I said, "I'd like to see those files." He hesitated for a moment, referring to the Data Protection Act. "The information they contain pertains to me, me personally," I pointed out. "The right to privacy isn't at issue here, so you can give me the files." Reluctantly, he retrieved them. "Go into the room over there, shut the door, and you can review them without anybody bothering you. I'll make copies of anything you need."

As I sat down and began leafing through the material, I found decrees, orders, directives, laws, Aryanization documents, and arrest warrants for Jews. The provincial manager of Arnsberg, the Dortmund office of the Gestapo, and the Schmallenberg town council had signed off on all of them. And they all had to have come across the desk of Amtsinspektor Holthaus. He had in fact signed a number of them. It was apparent that he had not only enriched himself personally, he had also been instrumental in organizing the pogrom (*Judenaktion*) in Schmallenberg in November 1938.

After scanning the material, I knocked on the door. "You can let me out now, Reinhold. I'm interested in more than just some of the documents—I'm interested in all of them."

After consulting with his superiors he told me that he would make me a copy of the file but that I had to promise in writing that the materials were strictly for my personal use and that I wouldn't disclose the information to others. I signed without a moment's hesitation— but, of course, I didn't keep my promise.

As I studied the files in more detail I came across a so-called "Jews' list" on which the name Selma Sara Frankenthal appeared twice. Since I knew only one Jewish woman by that name in Schmallenberg— Uncle Julius's wife's, Selma Frankenthal—I couldn't figure out what was going on. I thought about it for quite some time until I realized that the document was referring to Selma Friedrich, née Frankenthal, my father's sister. Somebody—probably Holthaus—had entered her on the list as a so-called "full Jewess" (*Volljüdin*), even though she was married to Karl Friedrich, an "Aryan," and had two "half-Aryan" sons.

As a "woman regarded as a Jewess" (*Geltungsjüdin*) or a "privileged Jewess" (*privilegierte Jüdin*), Aunt Selma would as a matter of course have been spared any persecution until late 1944.[11] But because her name appeared on the list, she was forced to wear the Star of David and was deported from Dortmund to Theresienstadt with the first transport in 1942. She was the only Schmallenberg or Dortmund Jew in that transport to survive the war. The only reason she wasn't deported from Theresienstadt to Auschwitz was probably that she had indicated the names of her "Aryan" relatives when she went through the registration process.

If Aunt Selma had died, Holthaus could have been charged with being an accessory to murder. Needless to say, I would've taken great pleasure in bringing the charges. Furious, I phoned Holthaus and quoted from some of the directives and decrees that bore his signature.

"And you mean to tell me that to this day you claim 'we had nothing to do with this whole Jewish business'?"

Holthaus's wife Hildegard could probably tell from his reaction to my call how angry I was. She walked over to the phone, took the receiver, and started talking to me: "What's this all about, Hans?"

"Your husband was a filthy swine, Hildegard!"

I told her everything I knew and said I found it difficult to imagine that being Holthaus's wife she had no knowledge of what he had done. I kept on hollering at her. "Maybe you'd better keep your mouth shut, because there are still things in your house that were once the property of Jews." Residents of Schmallenberg with whom I had discussed the files and Holthaus's role in seizing Jewish property had told me as much.

With all the fury I could muster, I accused of her lying. To top it all, she asked in utter innocence: "What are you talking about?"

"You have Uncle Sally's chest, a very valuable old chest, and a lot of other things besides. I have no idea how they came into your possession. But in any case, they're in your home now, and I'd like to have them back."

"I have a document to prove they were acquired legally. I'll go get it and read it to you."

The gist of the document was as follows: I, Sally Frankenthal, hereby entrust Frau Holthaus with such and such items for safekeeping, on the condition that she immediately surrender said items upon the return to Schmallenberg of any member of my family. As a member of the Nazi Party, Franz Holthaus himself probably didn't dare act as a trustee for a Jew.

"Isn't a nephew close enough to be considered a family member?" I asked her. "Besides, we have a certificate of inheritance that entitles us to Sally Frankenthal's belongings. I want the chest here in my house in twenty-four hours."

She asked me to do her the favor of allowing her to keep the chest for one more month. She said she wanted to try to find a similar one so that she wouldn't have to feel ashamed if people asked her about it.

"You're very fortunate," I told her. "I'm going to a health spa tomorrow, and I'll be back in four weeks. But the day after I come back, I want you to return everything you have that belongs to the Frankenthals."

When I called her after I got back she tried to delay the matter further; however, my patience had run out. "Not one hour longer—right now!"

"How do you expect me to get the things over to you?"

"There's a furniture store in your neighborhood. They have enough moving vans and men to do the job."

When she realized I wasn't joking, she quickly consented to have the Frankenthals' belongings removed from her house.

I immediately phoned her neighbors. "I know you all enjoy looking out your windows. Well, I just wanted to let you know that in an hour or so there's going to be something interesting happening in your neighborhood."

"OK—what is it?"

"You'll see."

It gave me a great sense of satisfaction to know the neighbors would witness the fact that more than forty years after the event, items belonging to Schmallenberg's Jews were being removed from the Holthaus home.

Franz Holthaus himself never responded to my accusations. Later, journalists rang his doorbell several times and tried to ask him what he knew about actions taken against Jews in Schmallenberg. But he just slammed the door in their faces and refused to answer their questions.

Shortly before Holthaus retired, I found out that he was going to get a promotion. As I sat with Mayor Falke and some friends in my favorite tavern, which I usually did on weekends, I couldn't restrain myself and suddenly shouted at the top of my voice: "Don't you people have any sensitivity at all? This man has committed so many crimes and has so many skeletons in his closet. And what do you do? You give him a promotion four weeks before he's scheduled to retire, so that he'll get even more money than he's entitled to now."

And what was the mayor's response? "We had no idea, Hans."

"You've been the mayor here for twenty years," I grumbled. "The least you could've done was to go over to the archives and ask whether the town had kept a file on Schmallenberg's Jews after the Nazis came to power!"

The Brochure

I made a great deal of use of what I learned from going through the files. Working with the various documents, I began to understand more about the administrative activity that went on between Berlin, the Dortmund office of the Gestapo, and the lower-level authorities in Schmallenberg. I now knew that anyone who had remained in an administrative position after 1945 and said he didn't know anything about the crimes committed by the Nazis was a liar.

I copied a number of documents and sent them to people's homes with the following note: "I knew nothing. I did nothing. I'm a decent person."

Afterward a lot of people suddenly began to admit that they had known or suspected most of what was going on at the time. As usual, however, the town council had no reaction to the revelations.

When Helga Tröster showed several residents of Schmallenberg, including me, her completed paper, Josef Wiegel, a teacher in the town, came up with the idea of publishing the results of her research in the form of a brochure. He approached the town council and then the local rifle club, which published the *Schmallenberger Heimatblätter.*

At first Schmallenberg's notables supported the project, but after they read the paper more carefully, Wiegel's telephone started ringing off the hook.

He told me that the material would be published only if certain passages were deleted.

"I haven't read the paper myself," I said. "But if it were up to me, I wouldn't change a word."

Helga Tröster felt the same as I did.

Nevertheless, the introduction to the paper was deleted. Tröster had quoted Frenn Wiethoff, a well-respected local historian who in the 1930s had expressed his views on Jews and the "racial" issue in general. Although he had been killed in the war, the town wanted to make sure that his name didn't appear in the brochure. Otherwise it would have been more difficult to continue publishing his works.

This didn't end the matter, however. Wiegel phoned me to emphasize the fact that the publisher didn't want to print the names of persons who had bought houses belonging to Jews.

"Well, why not?" I asked. "There's probably hardly a person in Schmallenberg who doesn't know their names already."

"That's true. But some of the buyers were members of the rifle club. In fact, they're still members today."

"Those are precisely the ones who should be mentioned by name."

"All right. But one of those who would be affected, for instance, would be the son of Tigges, the SA leader."

"Yes, well, I'm sorry for the boy. He's really a pretty decent fellow. But I don't feel sorry for the father. The buyers should be mentioned by name. And that's how I feel about it."

A few days later my telephone rang again. "Hans, I'd like to suggest a compromise."

"I'm all ears."

"What if we simply black out the names of the buyers?"

My answer came like a shot—I instantly agreed with Wiegel's proposal. No sooner had I hung up the phone than I dialed Helga Tröster's number. I asked her to join with Wiegel and me and gave her my reasons. "Look, the average reader probably isn't going to pay much attention to this business about the buyers anyway. They're certainly not going to worry about it. But what if they suddenly came across the following statements on a page: Max Frankenthal's house was acquired by—name blacked out. Sally Frankenthal's house together with Emil Frankenthal's attached butcher shop was acquired by—name blacked out. The house belonging to Max and Emil Stern was acquired by—named blacked out. Anybody who doesn't know the names already is going to ask questions. So please say yes."

Helga Tröster gave her consent and the brochure went to press.[12]

As soon as it appeared, the telephone lines wouldn't stop buzzing. The brochure had caused quite a stir. I got angry phone calls from people telling me that I had deliberately had the names blacked out and that I knew exactly what the response would be. With a smile on my face, I had to agree that they were right.

Moving to Dortmund

One day while I was still commuting between Schmallenberg and Dortmund on the weekends, Wolfgang Pollak, a member of the local Jewish community, took me aside after services and asked me to ride with him in his car.

We drove to an apartment on Ruhrallee. The woman who had been leasing it had died two weeks earlier and it was now available. Thinking I was just going to spend my weekends there, I decided to rent it. For a while I continued to stay in Schmallenberg during the week. Then I finally moved my furniture and myself to Dortmund.

However, I kept my Schmallenberg residence as my primary address. When people asked me why I still drove around with Sauerland plates on my car, I would answer them: "I don't want to see them put up a big sign at the entrance to the town."

"What kind of sign?"

"Schmallenberg is *judenrein* [free of Jews]! As long as I'm alive, I won't do them the favor."

Beginning in 1986, I took an increasing interest in the Jewish community. Under the aegis of the Society of Christians and Jews (Christlich-Jüdische Gesellschaft), I began to study the history of the Nazi persecution of the Jews, especially in Dortmund. Of the Jews who had lived in this city before 1933, none of those who returned had been old enough in the 1930s to remember what conditions had been like during the Nazi period.

In 1988 the Regional Association of the Jewish Communities of North Rhine–Westphalia (Landesverband der jüdischen Gemeinden von Nordrhein–Westfalen) asked me if I was interested in making sure that the Jewish cemeteries in the district of Arnsberg were being properly maintained. I told the Landesverband that I was, and a year later I was made responsible for all the 240 abandoned cemeteries in Westphalia.

The first thing I did was to inspect them. Whenever I discovered that they weren't being properly maintained—which was more often than not the case—I contacted the municipal authorities. A year later I made follow-up visits.

You can't imagine the condition that some of them were in. Marsberg, for example, had five Jewish cemeteries. Only one was being kept up; the others were completely neglected. I filed a complaint and waited a year, only to discover that in the meantime nothing had been done. After several attempts I finally reached the town clerk by phone. "Give me a break," he told me. "We've got five Jew cemeteries to take care of in Marsberg."

"First of all, they're called Jewish cemeteries. And second, the funds you receive are more than adequate to take care of all of them."

When I found out that this man wanted to become chairman of the regional council in Arnsberg, I made sure his plans didn't come to fruition.

It takes a lot of time to see to the preservation of so many cemeteries. On top of that, I was elected to the board of the Jewish community in Hagen and appointed vice president of the Landesverband. Consequently I was finding it increasingly difficult to cope with all my various duties.

I also visit schools once or twice a week to hold discussions with young people. These visits were triggered by an invitation I had received to give a talk about my past at an in-service for teachers. Because of their very positive response to my presentation, the teachers recommended me to other groups. Now I regularly speak in public about my life and my experiences during the Nazi period.

I once talked about Franz Holthaus to a group of teachers and principals from the Sauerland. During a break in the session, a teacher came up to me and said: "You keep mentioning this Holthaus person in Schmallenberg. The name of our principal happens to be Holthaus and he comes from Schmallenberg."

If his first name is Uli, I said, he's probably Franz Holthaus's son. When he asked if he had my permission to pass on the stories I had told, I said that he did.

Later, Uli Holthaus phoned me and accused me of saying horrible things about his father. My stories, he said, had actually reached the school of which he was the principal and he refused to tolerate the situation any longer. I told him that everything I had said about his father was a matter of record. I had copies of the files and they were also available at the courthouse in Schmallenberg.

He was furious. "What you're saying can't possibly be true. As a matter of fact, my father was an anti-fascist. When he was transferred to Olpe, his superior issued him a certificate stating that he had been an opponent of National Socialism. I saw it myself on his desk at the time."

What Franz Holthaus had gotten from his boss was what many Germans ironically call a *Persilschein,* or "denazification certificate," that is, a clean bill of health that absolved a person of all responsibility for his actions during the Nazi period.[13] I told his son that the certificate was a sham and that he was welcome to go to Schmallenberg and find out for himself what crimes his father was guilty of. Whenever I give a talk at a school, I always conclude by appealing to the young people. "Make sure that what happened to us, what took place in Germany, never happens again."

If a question-and-answer period has been scheduled, I add the following request: "Talk with your grandparents about what you've learned from listening to me. Ask them what they knew and what they did."

The only thing that parents and grandparents usually told their children and grandchildren was how they had escaped from the east, how they had fled from the "Soviets." If a young person refused to let up and kept hammering away at them, he or she invariably got a violent response. One young student told me that her grandfather warned her: "If you don't stop asking questions right now, I'll disinherit you." Another girl reported that after she had questioned her grandfather, he took a bottle of schnapps and disappeared into the chicken coop to get drunk. To me, responses such as these indicate personal knowledge of or perhaps even participation in criminal acts.

Many Germans I meet have never faced up to the past; it was much easier for them to repress it. Once, the local parish asked me to guide a group of seniors through the Anne Frank exhibit in Dortmund. As we stood near some photographs showing signs that read "Germans, defend yourselves—don't buy from Jews," I drew the group's attention to them. "All of you must remember seeing these signs. So let me ask you a question: Did a Jew ever force an 'Aryan' in Germany to buy at a Jewish-owned shop?" Half of the group, numbering about fifty, immediately left the exhibit, which to me was tantamount to a confession of guilt. By simply disappearing, they avoided the embarrassment of having to apologize to me.

"Now you see," the priest told me later, "how the generation of the perpetrators reacts when you talk about their evil deeds."

Occasionally I even receive threatening letters.

I generally make a distinction between the various generations. First, there is the generation of the perpetrators—and here I include the bystanders as well. Then there is the postwar generation, which felt obliged to ask questions about what had happened before their time. They defied their elders a little in 1968, but their protests didn't really amount to much. I'm now getting to know the third generation through my visits to various schools. This generation, finally, has a genuine desire to learn about the past.

An Unexpected Reunion

In the mid-1980s while I was reading the *Allgemeine Jüdische Zeitung,* I came across an invitation to help establish an Auschwitz committee in Hamburg.

I accepted the invitation and was promptly elected vice chairman.

Since that time, I've been closely involved with the committee, which is mainly concerned with preserving the memory of Auschwitz.

In the summer of 1986 I was riding the train back to Dortmund, returning from a meeting of the board in Hamburg. There was a young woman sitting in my compartment. She seemed quite shy and I assumed she was from East Germany. When the conductor came by to validate our tickets, it turned out that she hadn't paid the supplementary charge to travel on an intercity train. She was very frightened, so I gave her a little money and we got into conversation with each other. She told me that she came from Hagenow near Ludwigslust in East Germany. When I learned where her hometown was, I got an idea.

"Look, I have a friend in Ludwigslust and I would very much like to see him again. Do you think you could help me locate him?" I always carried a picture of him with me and took it out of my wallet. She examined the man in the photograph—Ede Besch—very carefully and promised to get in touch with me.

The last time I had heard anything about Ede was after the war, when his father contacted Ernst and me and asked us to help his son. Ede had been arrested in the Soviet occupation zone. Someone there had informed against him, saying that he had beaten prisoners in Monowitz. Although Ede could easily intimidate others by yelling at them, we never saw him lay a hand on anyone. Ernst and I swore an affidavit and sent it to his father. It eventually helped secure Ede's release. In 1947 I sent Ede a copy of my wedding photo. That was the last time we were in contact with each other.

The nice young lady from Hagenow phoned me a few days later. She worked in the city's cultural office and called me from her place of work. "I found Ede Besch! In the telephone directory—he actually has a phone. . . ."

Surprised, I asked her: "What do you mean, 'he actually has a phone'?"

"He must be a prominent politician or an SED man.[14] Otherwise he wouldn't have his own telephone," she explained to me indulgently. I didn't know a lot about the German Democratic Republic.

I asked her for an invitation so I could enter the GDR. As soon as it arrived, I got in my car and drove to Ludwigslust.

No sooner did I ring the bell on the little garden gate in front of Ede's house than a woman opened the door wide. "Hans!" she shouted and rushed up to me. I had never seen the woman in my life before. She hugged me and introduced herself as Luise Besch, Ede's wife. I was stunned. When I asked her where she knew me from, she got my wedding photo from the living room. Ede talks about you often, she said.

Naturally I wanted to see Ede in person. But Luise hedged a bit when I inquired about him. I kept pressing her, however, until she finally let the cat out of the bag. Ede was the police chief of Schwerin.

It wasn't easy, she said, for someone in his position to meet with a West German. But she would let him know that I was here and told me to come back the following day after work. This would give Ede some time, she went on, to consider whether he should be at home when you drop by.

The next evening, as I stood nervously in front of the little gate, I saw Ede run across the garden to greet me. We gave each other a long hug and spent half the night comparing where life had taken us since we had been separated in Nordhausen. It was hard to say good-bye after our reunion. I visited Ede often in the following years.

We particularly enjoyed arguing about politics. I reproached him for defending the Berlin Wall. "If we hadn't built it," he countered, "you would've bled our country white." I refused to see his point. It was only after West Germany had absorbed the GDR that I understood the full meaning of his words. By then, however, Ede was dead.

One afternoon Luise called to tell me that Ede had had an accident. A fractured rib had punctured his lung. Ede died after two days in the hospital, before I was able to get an entry permit for the GDR.

During my subsequent visits to East Germany, Luise often showed me the picture of his funeral.

Visiting Auschwitz

In May 1988 I went back to the place I had sworn I would never set foot in again. The Association of Persons Persecuted by the Nazi Regime (Die Vereinigung der Verfolgten des Naziregimes) was planning to hold a meeting in Auschwitz of former inmates from various countries. Members of the association urged me to attend. They kept on and on at me before I finally made up my mind.

Going back was extremely difficult.

I broke down at the International Monument commemorating the victims of fascism, even before entering the camp proper. I felt like leaving. The people I had come with could sense what was going on inside me and knew enough to leave me alone.

I began to feel better as I walked around Auschwitz I, the base camp, where I myself had never been before. I looked at the exhibits that a number of countries had put on display in the various blocks. I even managed to make an occasional comment. But as soon as we entered Auschwitz II, or Birkenau, I began to cry uncontrollably. I could barely tolerate the sight of the gas chambers and crematoria, where my parents and many other members of my family had been murdered.

I've never regretted making the journey, however. I still keep in touch with some of the young people from Hamburg who went with me to visit the camp.

During my stay in Poland I tried in vain to locate Jan Krupka. But aside from a number in a telephone directory—which nobody answered when I dialed it—I was unable to obtain any more information about him.

A year later I traveled to Poland again. On my second visit to Auschwitz I was irritated by the presence of so many symbols of Christianity at the site. I couldn't accept the fact that there were more crosses than Stars of David in Birkenau. The Poles who were in charge of the Auschwitz-Birkenau State Museum had erected the crosses. It had taken Israeli and American youngsters to put up the first Stars of David.

I went to Monowitz with a group of young people from the Auschwitz Committee. One can still get a sense of the size of the camp; remains of the barracks, the SS's air-raid shelter, and the main gate are still there. A small plaque with an inscription in English reminds visitors of the thirty thousand "anti-fascists" who were tortured to death. There is no mention that many of the prisoners were Jews.

As we walked around the factory grounds we met three men who lived in the Polish town of Monowice. We began talking with them and found out, among other things, that I. G. Farben had never compensated the Poles who had been expelled from Monowitz when construction began on the Buna plant or who had been deported to Germany as slave laborers.

In the West, I. G. Farben had been forced to reach a settlement after protracted negotiations. Anyone who had been a prisoner in the Buna works for more than six months was entitled to receive 5,000 DM.

The Association of Critical Shareholders—of which I am a member—still sends representatives to I. G. Farben's annual shareholders' meetings to try to raise the issue of compensation. Former slave laborers and prisoners living in Eastern Europe have yet to receive any reparations or to insist on their legal rights.

Whenever I spoke at meetings such as these, the sparks would fly. The "uncritical" shareholders didn't want to hear anything at all about the subject. They shouted: "Stop," "We know all about that," "That's the last straw—we suffered too," or "When are we going to get our factory in Auschwitz back?"

Once, they even switched off my microphone. Given the strength of my vocal cords, it didn't do them much good.

The Trial in Siegen

The trial of Ernst August König, a resident of Berleburg, took place in Siegen in 1987. König was charged with having committed crimes in the so-called Gypsy camp at Birkenau. I attended the proceedings so that I could give a report to the Hamburg Auschwitz Committee. The Jews in the Sauerland had always had good relations with the Sinti and Roma. When I was a child I often saw the Gypsy basket weavers repairing baskets for the butchers in Schmallenberg. And I used to bicycle past the large Gypsy colony near Berleburg on the way to my bar mitzvah lessons with Herr Stern. Although the Sinti and Roma were citizens of Berleburg, they were subjected to a great deal of prejudice. When they came to town to sell or peddle their wares, people would say: "Take your wash in. The Gypsies are here."

Although I had no personal knowledge of the Gypsies' having stolen anything, anti-Gypsy prejudice was as deep-seated as the anti-Semitism directed against us. Perhaps that's why we got along so well with each other.

In February 1943 the approximately twenty thousand Sinti and Roma living inside Germany's pre–World War II boundaries were deported to Birkenau, where they were imprisoned in the "Gypsy family camp." Most died a painful death. In August 1944 the Nazis gassed the some three thousand Gypsies who were still alive.

Ernst August König had been an SS Blockführer in the Gypsy camp at Birkenau.

One day during the trial, a former SS man by the name of Kühnemann was called as a defense witness. I was puzzled when I saw him enter the courtroom. The way he moved seemed strangely familiar to me. But I didn't really know who he was until he started to speak.

I became quite upset and talked to the public prosecutor during a recess in the proceedings. I told him that this was the same man who in March 1943 had killed Max Rosenstein's child by smashing its head against a pole.

Except for senior SS officers, we never knew the SS men by name. All we knew was that the murderer in this case was called "Graf" (the count). He haunted our thoughts in the camp. When Max Rosenstein worked in the kitchen in Monowitz and I was occasionally sent to

Birkenau, he would always ask me when I returned if I had seen "Graf."

When the public prosecutor asked the witness that afternoon if he had had a nickname at Auschwitz, he answered "Graf."

Ernst August König was sentenced to life in prison. Six months after the trial, he hanged himself in his cell.

The public prosecutor instituted preliminary proceedings against Kühnemann and subsequently filed charges against him. There were a number of witnesses for the prosecution. But in 1995, after the trial in Duisburg had gone on for nearly two years, the proceedings were postponed indefinitely because by that time Kühnemann was supposedly too old or too sick to stand trial.

Another Attempt at a Memorial

The town of Schmallenberg was eager to make up for the humiliation it had suffered as a result of the affair with the memorial stone commemorating the synagogue that had been burned down during Kristallnacht. So in 1987 the town council formed a committee to come up with some recommendations. The idea was to have a plaque with the names of the forty-four Jewish citizens of Schmallenberg who hadn't returned after the war.

Once again the town ignored me while another memorial was in the planning stage. I only found out about it through the Landesverband. An employee of the Landesverband phoned me to ask if I would go to Schmallenberg and get involved in the project.

"What exactly are you planning," I asked the committee members who had come up with the idea, "and where are you going to place the memorial?"

When they suggested the Jewish cemetery, I protested. "Under no circumstances. I've already had a stone put there for my parents and added an inscription 'for the forty-four Schmallenberg Jews who never returned.'"

The relatives of other Jewish families had had similar statements inscribed on headstones in the Jewish cemetery, which is why I refused to give my consent to the committee's plan. The committee members were anxious to get my approval, so they suggested another site for the plaque—the war memorial in the old Catholic cemetery. I asked them to wait until I had had a chance to inspect the site. Then I phoned them. "No way!" I said. "We're not going to have a Bitburg here in Schmallenberg." They asked me to explain, and so I continued: "I found the names of four or five men from Schmallenberg inscribed on the war memorial who were killed in action during the war. And I know for certain that they were all members of the Waffen SS. So it's simply out of the question."

At long last they asked if *I* had any ideas where to put the plaque. I suggested the place where the synagogue had stood. They warned me that it would be difficult to implement the project on that site. They felt certain that the current owner of the property wouldn't give us permission to place a memorial there. And they were right. He steadfastly refused to endorse our plan. I observed the charade for a while, and then I simply put some dummy memorials up. There were some more squabbles with the town—town officials said the memorials were too tall, for instance. The deliberations dragged on until January 1988, when Schmallenberg finally received its first memorial with the names of the Jews who had died in the Holocaust.

The Lahrmann Company

I managed to obtain 5,000 DM from I. G. Farben, which was part of the concern's "indemnification" for individuals "employed" as slave laborers. Smaller firms, however, such as the Lahrmann Company, which had also enriched themselves by exploiting Jewish slave labor, had gotten off scot-free. As early as the 1950s I had written to Ferdinand Lahrmann, pointing out that he had failed to pay his Jewish forced laborers the standard wage at the time of 80 pfennigs an hour. Instead, he had paid me 24 pfennigs, my brother 32 pfennigs, and the adult workers 56 pfennigs an hour. Needless to say, Jewish forced laborers had no right to be reimbursed for travel expenses or receive any other benefits. In other words, it was a good deal for Lahrmann.

I wasn't interested in getting money from him. What I wanted was a public declaration that spelled out how his company had exploited Jewish forced laborers and subjected them to intolerable working conditions. But my attempt to obtain an out-of-court statement from Lahrmann failed. He simply refused to issue one. The next step—to have the district court in Arnsberg decide the issue—also failed because, according to the court, the matter came under the statute of limitations.

1995: Fifty Years after My Liberation

In 1995 I went to Auschwitz to be present at ceremonies marking the fiftieth anniversary of the camp's liberation. As our bus drove through a Polish town, our interpreter pointed out a square where a monument to a marshal of the Soviet Union had once stood. "We tore it down and sent it back to Moscow and renamed the street that bore his name," she said proudly. Outraged, I walked to the front of the bus, spoke into the microphone, and asked her: "Aren't you ashamed? Who liberated you from the Nazis? It was the Russians, wasn't it!"

The rewriting of history that has been taking place during the past several years isn't confined to Poland. From the time in 1985 that West German Chancellor Helmut Kohl managed to get President Ronald Reagan to lay a wreath at the cemetery in Bitburg, where members of the Waffen SS are buried, there have been numerous attempts to play down the history of the "Third Reich." The survivors of the Holocaust were particularly affected by the dedication of the Neue Wache in Berlin, which is to serve as a "national" monument to "all victims of war and tyranny"—a memorial, in other words, that puts the perpetrators and their victims on the same level.[15]

Germans in general continue to avoid dealing with the crimes they committed. On the contrary, time and again I've had to listen to people expound the myth of the Wehrmacht and its "clean record" during the war. There was only one time in Schmallenberg that an acquaintance of mine told the truth about the Wehrmacht. It happened sometime in the late 1980s. I was having an argument in a tavern over the role of the Wehrmacht in the extermination of the Jews when Josef Brüggemann got up from the table and motioned me to follow him. In the toilet he confessed to me that my accusations were correct and that he himself had been a witness to crimes committed by soldiers of the Wehrmacht. When I questioned him further he told me that he had been stationed at a post in Poland behind the front lines. Yet he kept hearing machine-gun fire for days on end. Having grown increasingly suspicious, he headed in the direction from which the bursts of machine-gun fire were coming. With his own eyes he saw

Jews standing naked at the edge of a gravel pit being shot to death, while the Wehrmacht was cordoning off the area.

I wondered whether I should go back to the tavern and tell the others, "Well, here's your witness." I knew that Josef Brüggemann had been honest with me because we were very good friends. During the Nazi period when the farmers had stopped dealing with us openly, he would sometimes go and retrieve our livestock for us. And since I didn't want to cause him any embarrassment in the tavern, I decided not to say anything.

There isn't a single member of the Wehrmacht who can tell me he didn't know anything. When the Germans were retreating from Russia, they must have been struck by the fact that the towns they were passing through didn't have more than 10 percent of their former inhabitants. I'm convinced that the entire rank and file knew something about the butchery that had taken place. Much more will come to light in the years ahead. But we probably won't have the satisfaction of seeing the Germans finally own up to the crimes they committed.

My friends who fought on the front line sometimes say with regret that if Germany hadn't been sabotaged, it might never have lost the war. So I think that if I had told them what we had done at Auschwitz and Dora/Nordhausen to disrupt the war effort, they might have killed a Jew like me even long after the conflict had ended.

Ignorance about our history finds expression in many ways. On the fiftieth anniversary of our liberation in 1995, the southern ends of the main tunnels in Mittelbau-Dora were reopened and made accessible to the public. This was done to remind them of the underground V-2 rocket factories and of the suffering endured by the prisoners who were forced to labor in them. At the same time, there was an attempt to put on an exhibit of the rockets produced at the Peenemünde Research Station and to use the opening ceremony as an occasion to celebrate the beginning of rocket experimentation and the rocket industry in Germany. Nobody, of course, intended to show the conditions under which the rockets had been built. It was only because of pressure from survivors that the exhibit never opened. Nowadays rocket science is taken for granted. Most people admire the magnificent pictures broadcast from outer space on their television sets without thinking for a moment how and where these kinds of rockets were developed and how many concentration camp inmates had to pay for the original rocket program with their lives.

I visited Nordhausen and Mittelbau-Dora several times shortly before and after the fall of the Berlin Wall in 1990. The Treuhand wished to sell off the part of the Hartz Mountain region where the tunnels were located, to the Wildgruber Baustoff Werke (WIKO GmbH).[16] WIKO planned to level the entire mountain through which the tunnels had been built. If WIKO had realized its plan, the company would have destroyed the very sites that now serve as memorials to the prisoners' suffering. Heinz Galinski—the head of the Central Council of Jews in Germany at the time and himself a former inmate at the Dora concentration camp—and I managed to persuade company officials to level just part of the mountain, but even this wasn't easy to accomplish. We knew that 181 corpses had been discovered in a closed-off tunnel after the war and that they were most likely the bodies of dead Jews. So we insisted that according to Jewish law the tunnel become an eternal resting place for them. So far our argument has been accepted. . . .

In the mid-1990s I went through a serious crisis. I felt that I simply couldn't go on any longer. I was only getting one or two hours' sleep a night and had terrible nightmares. Every evening when I went to bed, I thought to myself: "Hopefully you won't wake up in the morning."

The situation got so bad that I went to see a psychiatrist. She prescribed tranquilizers and sleeping pills for me. After a time I improved somewhat.

I might have committed suicide during this period of my life, but I have a great deal of respect for death. I've seen a number of my acquaintances die and witnessed the torment that Holocaust survivors go through as they depart this life. All their memories come back to them. It's simply horrible.

I'd like to be buried in Schmallenberg when I die. But someone will have to get special authorization and the Jewish cemetery will have to be reopened on that day. The whole thing is probably too complicated. The Jewish cemetery in Schmallenberg is built on a slope and my friends often kid me: "We'll never get a heavyweight like you up the hill." My friend Kurt Eppelmann came up with an excellent solution: "We can put a crane in Dr. Becker's garden, and I'll just slowly lower

Frankenthal into his grave. Then nobody'll have to carry him." Everyone agreed with Eppelmann.

We won't reach that point for quite some time to come, though. At the moment, I continue to work from morning till evening. I'm active in the Jewish community and am involved in preserving the memory of our persecution. I continue to visit schools and am busy with many other things besides. To my dying day I will always be a prisoner of what I've lived through. I'm nonetheless a happy person. On a recent trip to Israel I met someone and fell in love again. And I'm now enjoying the springtime. . . .

❀

Afterword

Babette Quinkert, Andreas Plake, and Florian Schmaltz

. . . in the house of the hangman one should not speak of the
noose, otherwise one might seem to harbor resentment.
—Theodor W. Adorno, "Was bedeutetet"

When Hans Frankenthal returned to Germany from Auschwitz he
found he did not have to speak of the noose and nonetheless met with
resentment. Like many other Holocaust survivors in the postwar era,
he encountered stubborn silence and psychological repression on the
part of those who had actively or passively participated in the persecution of the Jews. After Allied forces had defeated the terrorist Nazi
regime and opened the gates of the concentration camps, many survivors soon came to realize, with a sense of resignation, that the majority of Germans viewed liberation primarily as defeat and collapse.
Adorno's assessment in the late 1950s—"the oft-invoked working
through of the past has to this day been unsuccessful and has degen-
erated into its own caricature, an empty and cold forgetting"—has
lost none of its relevance to the current situation. Nor has the social
criticism embodied in his conclusion that the reason for this is "that
the objective conditions of society that engendered fascism continue
to exist."[1]

Indifference, psychological repression, silence, and denial were
widespread. Until the 1980s, commemorations of the victims of the
Nazi regime were confined to a committed minority in West German
society. And the fact that various aspects of the Nazi regime have in
recent years been singled out as topics for public discussion has not
necessarily given rise to a critical analysis of the societal causes of the
crimes that were committed. A not inconsiderable number of popular

interpretations have been shaped by a resuscitated theory of totalitarianism that is ultimately nothing more than an attempt to relativize the crimes of the Nazis. Breaking taboos has provoked sharp controversies, as in the case of the Hamburg Institute for Social Research's traveling exhibition on the Wehrmacht's participation in crimes committed in the occupied territories during World War II.[2] And the further breaking of taboos continues to engender bitter opposition and hostility.

Despite wide-ranging debates, many of the surviving victims of forced-labor camps and concentration and extermination camps still have difficulty finding an audience for their points of view and their concerns. Fifty-plus years after liberation, the number of those who are able to report firsthand about the crimes committed against them is growing smaller and smaller. Therefore it is all the more important to document their memories.

The German Auschwitz Committee, where survivors meet with younger people to keep the memory of the victims of Auschwitz alive, initiated the proposal for Hans Frankenthal's autobiography.[3] Frankenthal subsequently accepted our invitation to record his life story. We interviewed him over several days, and followed up with additional interviews later. It was agreed among all that Babette Quinkert would put the autobiography together from the taped conversations with Frankenthal and craft the narrative. Andreas Plake and Florian Schmalz then worked in close cooperation with him to produce the final version. We adhered to Hans Frankenthal's stylistic technique of reproducing the words that he and others exchanged at the time, but we cannot of course ensure that they constitute a verbatim record of conversations that took place decades ago.

During the last years of his life, Hans Frankenthal tirelessly studied publications and research materials dealing with the history of Auschwitz. Thus he supplemented his personal memories with reflections on politics and history. To do justice to his concern with these topics, we decided to add a detailed glossary.

Hans Frankenthal's memoirs are a testament to the victims of Auschwitz and to the Resistance movement that more than once saved his brother's and his life. But there is another reason for their extraordinary importance. Since he was one of the few survivors of a community of Jews who lived and grew up in a rural environment, he was able to describe for us firsthand a social milieu that has disappeared forever from Germany. Today there is virtually nothing left to remind people of the history of the Jewish livestock dealers in whose world Hans Frankenthal grew up and from which he was so brutally snatched away. Finally, the story of his return to Schmallenberg in 1945 reveals how German society "came to terms" with its immediate past.

Hans Frankenthal's life is tied to the history of I. G. Farben and Buna plant no. 4 in a very special way. He spent most of his adolescent years as a prisoner and slave laborer in Farben's own concentration camp at Monowitz. The way in which I. G. Farben has dealt with its past and the issue of compensating the prisoners it exploited is a perfect illustration of the way Germans have, as they put it, "mastered" the past. Hans Frankenthal, whose life was forever scarred as a result of his imprisonment and the persecution to which he was subjected, continued until his death in 1999 to work to enlighten people about I. G. Farben's involvement in genocide.

I. G. Auschwitz under Indictment

At the end of the Second World War, nearly half of I. G. Farben's total work force of 330,000 was made up of people "employed" against their will: slave laborers, prisoners of war, and concentration camp inmates.[4] A widespread myth persists that the utilization of slave labor by large corporations such as I. G. Farben occurred within the framework of cruel and inhuman regulations imposed by the Reich government. This was what Farben representatives contended in their defense during the postwar trial of war criminals at Nuremberg, where count three of the indictment charged them with participation in a "slave-labor program." Like members of the Wehrmacht, I. G. Farben executives sought to justify their actions by invoking what has been termed the defense of necessity. Despite a wealth of evidence to the contrary, a majority of the court accepted the defendants' argument and acquitted them of the charge of slavery and mass murder—with one exception: I. G. Auschwitz and Fürstengrube, a nearby I. G. coal mine where slave labor was used. Here the court wasted no time in dismissing the defense of necessity:

> As we recapitulate the record of Auschwitz and Fürstengrube, we find that these were wholly private projects operated by Farben, with considerable

freedom and opportunity for initiative on the part of Farben officials connected therewith. The evidence does not show that the choice of the Auschwitz site and the erection of a Buna and fuels plant thereon were matters of compulsion, although favored by the Reich authorities, who were anxious that a fourth Buna plant be put into operation.

The court went on to express itself in the clearest possible language:

> The use of concentration camp labor and forced foreign workers at Auschwitz, with the initiative displayed by the officials of Farben in the procurement and utilization of such labor, is a crime against humanity and, to the extent that non-German nationals were involved, also a war crime, to which the slave-labor program of the Reich will not warrant the defense of necessity. It also appears that the employment of concentration camp labor was had with knowledge of the abuse and inhumane treatment meted out to the inmates by the SS, and that the employment of these inmates on the Auschwitz site aggravated the misery of these unfortunates and contributed to their distress.[5]

Still, only five of the officials responsible for I. G. Auschwitz were given prison sentences under count three. Otto Ambros and Walther Dürrfeld were sentenced to eight years each, Fritz ter Meer to seven, and Carl Krauch and Heinrich Bütefisch to six years each. Even before they had finished serving their sentences, the Farben executives were free men again and soon rose to high positions in the West German chemical industry.

Alms for Prisoners: The Question of Compensation

By the time the judges in Nuremberg handed down their verdicts in the I. G. Farben trial on 29 and 30 July 1948, the Allied Control Council already had legal title to all Farben's assets. The Allies were intent on the dismantling and dismemberment of the company to prevent Germany from remilitarizing in the future. Farben's assets were to be divided among nine companies, including BASF, Bayer, Hoechst, and Casella. Before the formal dissolution of Farben was complete, however, the firm continued to exist as "I. G. Farbenindustrie AG in Liquidation" (I. G. Farben i. L.) to protect the successor companies from creditors' claims. Paying off Farben's creditors and ensuring that former Farben employees received their pensions played an important part in the negotiations between the Allies and representatives of German companies and banks on dissolving the former chemical giant. But the question of compensating the surviving prisoners of Monowitz went by the boards.[6] The first time a West German court dealt with the question was when Norbert Wollheim, a former prisoner at Monowitz, filed a lawsuit against I. G. Farben i. L. On 3 November 1951 Henry Ormond, Wollheim's lawyer, submitted a claim for damages in the amount of 10,000 DM as compensation for nonpayment of wages for the twenty-two months of labor Wollheim had been forced to perform at the construction site of the Buna plant in Auschwitz.[7] The claim covered damages for the pain and suffering incurred as a result of Farben's deliberate failure to take precautions to protect its conscripted workers. Ormond, by the way, had himself been an inmate at Dachau in 1938.

This was the first trial in which a West German court dealt with German industry's responsibility for the suffering incurred by slave laborers and with the issue of compensating them for their treatment. The case established a precedent for the way the West German judiciary—as well as industry, the government, and various government agencies—would deal with the victims of the forced-labor system in subsequent decades.

The trial opened on 16 January 1952 in the Frankfurt am Main district court (*Landgericht*). Former concentration camp inmates and British POWs who had also been used as slave laborers by I. G. Farben testified about conditions in Monowitz. They described the continual hunger, the prevalence of disease, and the brutal treatment meted out by the SS and the Farben foremen at the construction site. They also described how prisoners who were no longer considered fit for work would be selected for extermination. Witnesses for the defense denied the existence of such conditions so vehemently that the judges felt compelled to reprimand "the defendants and their people for their appalling indifference to the plaintiff and the imprisoned Jews." Such indifference was comprehensible only if one assumed that the responsible persons at I. G. Farben "truly regarded Jewish prisoners as inferior human beings and not as employees whose welfare they were obliged to provide for."[8]

The court found that I. G. Farben had offered no resistance to the SS's treatment of prisoners, "which it could have done within certain limits . . . if it had wished to" and that it was therefore guilty of failure to render assistance. The court determined further that the representatives of the concern had undertaken no "serious attempts" to improve "the lot of the plaintiff or [other] Jewish prisoners." Hence it decided that the plaintiff had proved culpable bodily harm and that Wollheim's request for damages of 10,000 DM was fair and reasonable.[9]

The judgment reached in this "court of first instance" on 10 June 1953 appeared to signal a breakthrough in settling damage claims filed by individuals against German industrial enterprises. But German industry also recognized the huge significance of the trial. Former I. G. Auschwitz employees who in the meantime had found jobs with Farben's successor companies had carefully watched the Wollheim proceedings. In their internal reports they referred to it as a "clear test case that will be followed by an as yet indeterminable number of lawsuits filed by other [former] camp inmates or their heirs against [German] businesses."[10] By the fall of 1952, eleven hundred survivors had already gotten in touch with Ormond's law office or had contacted I. G. Farben's attorneys directly as a result of the enormous publicity produced by the trial.[11]

Industry representatives and government bureaucrats feared the consequences of a verdict in favor of the plaintiff. So even before the judgment was announced, they began discussing possible strategies to deal with the flood of lawsuits that would be filed by other former slave laborers against German industrial firms. In May 1953 the Farben liquidators met with representatives of Krupp, Mannesmann, various iron and steel companies, officials of the Ministry of Finance, and representatives from the Federal Chancellor's Office who were responsible for judicial, labor, and domestic matters. Also present was a member of the Federal Association of German Industry (Bundesverband der Deutschen Industrie). German business forged a consensus on rejecting any claims for compensation.[12] They aggressively pushed for laws to protect German industry from future lawsuits filed by former concentration camp prisoners. And later, the industry lobby frequently involved itself in the deliberations on amending the Federal Indemnification Law (Bundesentschädigungsgesetz, or BEG).[13]

In August 1953 the liquidation committee took a harder line with

Economics Minister Ludwig Erhard. It threatened to claim compensation from the Federal Republic as the National Socialist regime's legal successor if the West German government recognized claims filed by former concentration camp inmates against I. G. Farben.[14] On 3 December 1954 an industry representative at the hearings held by the Bundestag committee responsible for indemnification once again referred to the Wollheim case. He called upon the parliament to amend the BEG and make the Federal Republic, as the legal successor to the Nazi regime, liable for all damage claims filed by former slave laborers rather than the industrial enterprises that had "employed" them.[15]

In the spring of 1956, German big business modified its modus operandi. Gustav Stein, general manager (*Hauptgeschäftsführer*) of the Federal Association of Germany Industry, addressed the organization's concerns with the state secretary under Konrad Adenauer in the Federal Chancellor's Office. The man who held that post at the time was no less a personage than Hans Globke, the coauthor of a commentary on the Nuremberg Laws. Stein told Globke that the "conclusion of a settlement à la Wollheim *v.* I. G. Farben i. L with organizations representing persecutees" was now being promoted by the industry side "for foreign policy reasons." Stein went on to explain that in changing course, German companies sought to avoid "extensive proceedings during which a number of respected American citizens who had at one time been imprisoned in a concentration camp would be called to the witness stand to give evidence." Aside from the foreign policy risk that "the examination of these witnesses would take place in the United States and adversely affect our image in that country," Stein was also afraid that the Germans could suffer material losses as a result. The hearing, he said, "would jeopardize our efforts to recover German property."[16] In order to find a solution, the German ambassador in Washington, Heinz Krekeler, was brought into the process.[17]

In the end, prominent American Auschwitz survivors were not subpoenaed as witnesses. After being contacted by thousands of survivors, Henry Ormond had sought support from the Jewish organizations that had gotten involved in the difficult negotiations. On 5 February 1957 the Farben liquidators signed an agreement with the Conference on Jewish Material Claims Against Germany. It provided for a fund of 30 million DM to compensate victims of forced labor at I. G. Farben's Monowitz and Heydebreck plants in Upper Silesia and the Fürstengrube and Janina coal mines.[18] When the agreement came into effect, the judgment in the Wollheim case was to be annulled. Before that happened, however, two conditions had to be met. First, the Bundestag had to pass a special law (*Aufrufgesetz*) setting time limits for filing claims on Farben's assets.[19] And second, the agreement had to be approved at a general meeting of I. G. Farbenindustrie's stockholders.

After the conditions had been met, a total of 5,855 Jewish survivors in forty-two countries received a one-time payment of 5,000 DM each, provided they had been at Monowitz for longer than six months. Those who had been forced to work for Farben between one and six months received a lesser amount. And the few survivors who had been "employed" by Farben for less than a month went away empty-handed. For the twenty-three months he had been imprisoned and had been forced to work in the Monowitz concentration camp, Hans Frankenthal also received 5,000 DM. Many former prisoners, however, were unable to claim compensation because by the time they learned about the indemnification agreement, the deadline for filing had passed.

I. G. Farben insisted that it had made the indemnification payments on a "voluntary" basis and that they could under no circumstances be used to support claims for compensation by individual concentration camp inmates. The liquidators wrote as follows with regard to the agreement: "When I. G. has finished paying the C. C. [Claims Conference], the C. C. shall give I. G. immunity from all future claims brought by [former] Jewish prisoners [seeking compensatory damages] as a result of their employment by I. G. Also, the C. C. will assume the cost of any future litigation involving [former] Jewish concentration camp inmates who refuse to agree to the settlement."[20]

The "indemnification" agreement negotiated in the context of the Wollheim trial pointed the way for all subsequent lawsuits filed against German companies. To this day, the position of German industry has remained fundamentally unchanged. Only under the pressure of claims brought by former concentration camp prisoners have companies that were involved in crimes at Auschwitz recognized that they have a certain moral obligation to help the victims. They continue, however, to dispute their political and legal responsibility, as well as the claims of individual survivors to compensatory damages.

They still seek to uphold a view of history that denies or relativizes the responsibility of German companies and their managers for the exploitation and murder of concentration camp inmates. Instead they speak of their "fateful entanglement" and of the oppressive coercion imposed upon them by the SS—as if the company representatives at Auschwitz were the victims. German industry intends to continue using this version of history as a means to fend off former concentration camp inmates seeking individual damage payments from private industry.

The original disposition to formally dissolve I. G. Farben lessened as the years passed. To the contrary, instead of compensating the surviving slave laborers and prisoners with the residual assets of a firm that had participated in genocide, in 1990 the liquidators demanded the return of Farben property expropriated by the GDR after World War II.[21]

Monowitz (Monowice) Today

Given its historical significance, the Monowitz concentration camp is surprisingly unknown. It has barely been studied and is seldom commemorated. The organizers of the Auschwitz Museum have paid relatively little attention to I. G. Farben's concentration camp. The exhibits in the blocks at the former base camp (*Stammlager*) contain just two references to Monowitz: a painted sketch of the camp on a large topographical wall map of the entire Auschwitz complex, and a list on display in a glass cabinet of prisoners selected in the Monowitz infirmary for extermination at Birkenau.

Most visitors take the museum tour of the base camp. Noticeably fewer walk two kilometers farther to Birkenau, where the remains of the extermination center convey a more powerful impression of the enormous dimensions of Auschwitz. Very few visitors ever get as far as Monowitz.

Those who do decide to visit the camp can reach the former Farben works from the town of Óswięçim. Near the main entrance to the modern chemical complex is a large memorial to the dead of Monowitz that was erected after a public appeal for donations in 1966. Taking the road south of the factory grounds eastward, you drive for several kilometers past the fence that surrounded the Buna works. This gives you a good idea of the mammoth size of the facilities that were once located on the other side. To the right, on the opposite side of the road, some bunkers and the remains of camp no. 6's gateposts are still visible. This is where twelve hundred British POWs were imprisoned from the autumn of 1943. A few hundred meters further on, after you pass a factory gate on your left, an access road leads to the village of Monowice. This is where the Monowitz concentration camp was built in 1942. A white stone cross with a plaque commemorating the victims of Monowitz has been placed along the former street that ran through the middle of the camp and that still divides the present-day village.

Even though the wooden prisoners' barracks no longer exist, you can still find remnants of the former camp. The brick "forge" that was used to store potatoes, the Blockführer's quarters, and a bombproof bunker for the camp guards have all survived intact. Several ruined structures still stand at the western edge of the village: two stone barracks used by the SS and a headquarters building for the camp commandant. These were part of the administrative complex located outside the fence that surrounded the camp. If you walk to the end of the four-hundred-meter-long street in the northeast sector of the camp, you can still see the autopsy room, next to the prisoners' infirmary. The only thing left of the electrified barbed-wire fence is a bent corner pillar made of concrete standing in the middle of a field at the extreme southeastern boundary of the former camp. The many half-underground bombproof bunkers where guards who were posted outside the camp sought cover during air raids reveal the contours of the camp's boundaries. Another large bunker located approximately a hundred meters to the south was also used for shelter during air attacks.

A sightseeing tour of Monowitz combined with further study of the concentration camp show how inextricably linked the base camp, Birkenau, and Monowitz were. One cannot help wondering to what extent Auschwitz had been built to serve the interests of I. G. Farben and what part the Birkenau extermination camp played as a ready source of cheap labor for the concern. Farben requested the SS to "select" from among the deportees the workers it needed. Then it proceeded to work them to death. Farben paid the SS a rental fee of 4 reichsmarks a day for skilled workers and 3 for unskilled laborers.

Prisoners averaged three months at Monowitz before Farben representatives declared them "unfit for work." Farbenindustrie also used slave laborers in the coal mines that secured the company's supply of energy. Under the dreadful conditions in the mines, a prisoner's chance of survival dropped to between four and eight weeks.

Farben arranged for the SS to replace its exhausted and ailing workforce with fresh inmates. "Unusable" prisoners were sent to Birkenau for extermination. Even at this point, however, Farben netted profits from its prisoners. The company had a 42.5 percent interest in Degesch, the firm that supplied the poison known as Zyklon-B that was used in the gas chambers.

Since the ranks of the eyewitnesses are growing thinner and thinner, Hans Frankenthal was afraid that there would soon be no one left to stop people from forgetting or to confront them with the crimes that were committed. It was his special wish that what is left of the camp not be allowed to fall further into disrepair. He hoped that the remains of the camp would be preserved in memory of the Jews and Poles of Monowitz who were expropriated and evicted from their homes as well as a memorial to the victims of "extermination by work" at I. G. Farben's installations. An exhibit at the site of the camp explaining what happened at Monowitz would add significantly to people's understanding of Auschwitz and help keep its memory alive.

❖

Translator's Notes

1. SA stands for Sturmabteilung, the paramilitary "storm trooper" units of the NSDAP, the Nationalsozialistische Deutsche Arbeiterpartei (National Socialist German Workers' Party), the official name of the Nazi Party; the members of the SA were also known as Brownshirts.

2. The Horst Wessel Song was the official anthem of the Nazi Party. The text came from a poem by SA Sturmführer Horst Wessel, whom the Nazis made into a martyr after his death on 23 February 1930. After 1933 the Horst Wessel Song became a second national hymn of the German Reich, regularly played after the national anthem, *Deutschland über alles*.

3. *Amtsinspektor* was a rank in the German civil service system; the person holding this rank could also exercise police functions.

4. The Kindertransport (Children's Transport) rescue effort was launched after Kristallnacht, when the British Parliament passed a resolution calling upon the government to open the gates of England to Jewish refugee children from Germany and Austria. With the support of Jewish and non-Jewish organizations, relief committees in Great Britain found foster families for them in Jewish and non-Jewish homes. The emigration departments of the central Jewish organizations in Germany chose the children who were to be sent. The children traveled to England by train via the Netherlands. By September 1939 some ten thousand children had reached Great Britain. However, thousands of other children who were in the process of escaping were trapped in the Netherlands when war broke out. After the Wehrmacht invaded Holland, they ended up in the clutches of the German occupiers.

5. An *Arbeitskolonne* was a segregated Jewish labor brigade or work gang.

6. The term *posel* derives from the Hebrew word for "disqualified" or "rejected" and is applied mainly to objects used for ritual purposes (such as the scroll of the Torah) that have not been made according to the strict requirements of Jewish law or that have been damaged or otherwise rendered unfit.

7. The word *ivrit*, "Hebrew," derives from the term usually applied to describe the early Israelites (*ivri*). For centuries Hebrew was primarily the language of prayer and theology and was used as a written language by scholars. During the Haskalah, or Jewish "enlightenment" (the period between 1784 and 1881), Hebrew was revived and once again became a spoken language. Thousands of new words had to be added to describe all the complex culture of modern life. Since 1948, *ivrit* has been the official language of the state of Israel.

8. *Loshn koydesh* (Yiddish) literally means "holy language," or Hebrew, but in this case "Lauschen-Kaudesch" probably refers to a mixture of German, Yiddish, and Hebrew.

9. The *Rampe* was the loading platform where those who arrived in Auschwitz were selected for forced labor or sent directly to the gas chambers.

10. The *Appell* was the roll call, which took place in the camp yard, or *Appellplatz* (roll-call square).
11. Kommandos were prisoner work squads, led by a Kapo (see glossary).
12. Buna is a brand of synthetic rubber.
13. The *Postenkette* consisted of the *große Postenkette*, or "large cordon," which enclosed the entire camp during the day, and the *kleine Postenkette*, or "small cordon," which at night occupied only the watchtowers and patrolled along the perimeter.
14. *Yeke* is a Yiddish word meaning "fool," derived from the German word *Gecke*. *Mame-Luschen*, or *mame-loshn*, or *mama loshen*, is a Yiddish term that literally means "mother tongue" and usually refers to Yiddish. In this case, though, it probably means a kind of pidgin Yiddish.
15. During the Nazi period the term "ethnic German" (*Volksdeutsch*) was applied to persons of German origin who did not have German citizenship and lived beyond the pre-1938 borders of the Reich and Austria. A decree of 29 March 1939 issued by the Reich Minister of the Interior defined an ethnic German as "a person who declares himself or herself to be a member of the German nation provided that said declaration can be confirmed on the basis of specific indicators such as language, upbringing, culture, etc. Persons of non-Germanic blood, especially Jews, can never be ethnic Germans even if they declare themselves such."
16. In the jargon of Auschwitz, prisoners who had been sent to the camp for "criminal offenses" were called "greens," because they were required to wear a green triangular badge on the left side of their chest and their trouser leg. The SS gave preference to greens when they appointed Kapos.
17. A *Lagerführer* (camp leader) was an SS officer who functioned as the standing representative of the commandant.
18. A *Rapportführer* was a noncommissioned SS officer (*Unterführer*) who occupied a position in the SS hierarchy somewhere between the camp leader (*Lagerführer*) and the SS block leaders (*Blockführers*) who were subordinate to him. He recorded prisoner population numbers and reported them and important goings-on in the camp to the camp leader.
19. These lower-level, generally younger prisoner-functionaries were appointed to aid the barrack-room chief, with responsibility for maintaining cleanliness in the barracks, bringing food and laundry, and seeing to the prisoners' clothing and fuel.
20. The *Lagerältesten* were the senior camp prisoners, the top prisoner-functionaries (see glossary); the responsible representatives of the prisoners vis-á-vis the camp leadership, and the highest-placed receivers of orders in the chain.
21. The Little Red Riding Hood and Little White Riding Hood Kommandos were women's work units, which performed their duties in the "Canada" section of Birkenau, where the *Effektenkammern* (storerooms of belongings), thirty-five special huts to sort and patch clothing and other articles and to store the possessions that the Jews had been robbed of at the loading platform, were located. The Kommandos' name was part of Auschwitz prisoners' jargon and came from the fact that the women wore colored headscarves. When Jews arrived at the camp, they were instructed to leave their valuables and luggage at designated spots on the loading platform. A so-called freight Kommando (*Rollkommando*), staffed by men, transported the loot to "Canada," where the Little Red Riding Hood and Little White Riding Hood Kommandos sorted it. This vast store of plundered clothing, valuables, suitcases, and household items got its name because in Poland, Canada was considered a land of boundless wealth.
22. A *Strafkompanie* was a punishment unit, a separate penal Kommando within the camps.
23. The Volkssturm was the "People's Storm Unit," a paramilitary formation set up in

October 1944 as the last-ditch defenders of the Reich. All men aged sixteen to sixty were organized in their local areas, with little training and few weapons, under the leadership of any available officers.

24. "Corduroy road" refers to a road formed of trees sawed in half longitudinally and laid transversely across a track. A road thus made presents a ribbed appearance, like that of corduroy. Corduroy roads were used by loggers to easily move cut timber down steep slopes and by the military to keep heavy cannons out of the mud.

PART 2

1. The Reichsarbeitsdienst (RAD) was a compulsory labor conscription program introduced in June 1935; it obliged all German men between the ages of nineteen and twenty-five to six months' labor service, mainly in agriculture and on public works projects. Later, women were also included in the RAD. Originally conceived as a means to combat unemployment, it developed into an instrument that prepared young people for war.

2. Stutthof was a Nazi concentration camp at the mouth of the Vistula River. It existed from 2 September 1939 to 9 May 1945. About 115,000 prisoners passed through Stutthof; of these, 65,000 perished, and 22,000 were moved to other concentration camps.

3. The Reichsnährstand (Reich Food Estate) was a monopoly organization established by law on 19 March 1933; it included all persons and businesses involved in agricultural production, cultivation, and processing as well as the marketing of farm products. Membership was obligatory. It was the organization that undergirded all National Socialist agricultural policy.

4. The KPD was the Kommunistische Partei Deutschlands (Communist Party of Germany).

5. CDU stands for Christlich-Demokratische Union (Christian Democratic Union) and is a German political party advocating regulated economic competition and close cooperation with the U.S. in foreign policy. The CDU held power in the Federal Republic of Germany from the establishment of the West German Republic in 1948 until 1969 and again from 1982 until 1998. It is a center-right party.

6. Besides his commentary on the Nuremberg Laws, Hans Globke (1889–1973) also had a part in writing a number of other laws used to further the persecution of Jews in Germany. These included a decree drafted in 1944 that regulated the transfer of the assets of dead (and murdered) Jews to the Reich. In the Federal Republic he became state secretary under Konrad Adenauer in the Chancellor's Office, a post he held until 1963 despite intense public criticism and the publication of incriminating Nazi documents in the German Democratic Republic. (Adenauer, a cofounder of the Christian Democratic party, was the first chancellor of postwar Germany [1949–66].)

Hans Filbinger (b. 1913) was forced to resign in 1977 as minister president (governor) of the state of Baden-Württemberg as a result of a press campaign led by the author Rolf Hochhuth. Filbinger had recommended in his doctoral dissertation four decades earlier that "racial inferiors" should be put to death and dangerous "moral criminals" castrated. It was also reported that he had signed death sentences for teenage naval deserters in the final days of the war. His public denials of these charges proved to be lies.

7. A schuetzenfest is a type of shooting match.

8. The American Jewish Joint Distribution Committee, or AJDC (popularly known as the JDC and the "Joint"), founded after the beginning of World War I, sought to help Jews wherever in the world they might be subjected to persecution or pogroms. During

World War II the organization focused its efforts on the persecuted Jews of Europe. Among other things, it distributed food and provided financial support for various relief schemes. After 1945 the AJDC emerged as the most important relief organization for survivors of the Holocaust. It is still among the largest and most important Jewish social welfare organizations.

9. The *Erbschein,* or certificate of inheritance, has no equivalent in Anglo-American law. It carries the strong presumption that the person to whom it has been issued has the right of inheritance. The certificate of inheritance is limited to objects. See *The German Civil Code* (as amended to January 1, 1992), and the *Introductory Act to the Civil Code of August 15, 1986* and the *Act on Liability of Defective Products of December 15, 1989,* translated with an introduction by Simon L. Goren (Littleton, Colo.: F. B. Rothman, 1994), Book 5: Eighth Section: Certificate of Inheritance, pp. 421–25.

10. The SPD is the Sozialdemokratische Partei Deutschlands (Social Democratic Party of Germany). The SPD is a center-left political party that calls for government control or regulation of large industry; it is Germany's oldest and largest single party. Outlawed by the Nazis in 1933, the SPD revived after WWII. The SPD joined a coalition with the Christian Democrats in 1966 and then in 1969 became senior partners in a coalition government with the Free Democrats (a German centrist party that advocates individualism and free economic competition). This coalition governed until 1982. In 1998 the SPD formed a coalition with the Green party to run Germany at the national level.

11. After the Reichstag passed the Gesetz zum Schutze des deutschen Blutes und der deutschen Ehre (Law for the Protection of German Blood and German Honor) on 12 September 1935, a complicated classification system was enacted defining various degrees of Jewishness. Anybody with four Jewish grandparents on the rolls of the Jewish community was considered a "full Jew." These rolls were similar to parish registers, and as I understand were kept by synagogues and/or boards of the various Jewish communities.

Geltungsjuden were persons regarded as Jews even though they had two "Aryan" grandparents. They were treated like full Jews (as if they had four Jewish grandparents), but they escaped the deportations to death camps and survived the war because they had non-Jewish family members. *Geltungsjuden* were without legal rights and were forced to wear the Star of David. "Privileged" marriages existed when the wife was Jewish or the couple had at least one child they had baptized as a Christian, rather than enrolled in a Jewish community. Jewish women married to German Gentile men were considered "Aryan" households and were designated by Hitler in 1938 as privileged intermarriages. Jews in privileged intermarriages did not wear the Star of David, and very few were arrested during the final roundup. See Nathan Stoltzfus, *Resistance of the Heart: Intermarriage and the Rosenstrasse Protest in Nazi Germany* (New York: Norton, 1996), pp. 102–3, 155, 301n, 304n.

12. The brochure, titled *Geschichte und Schicksal der Juden in Schmallenberg* (History and Fate of the Jews in Schmallenberg), was published in Schmallenberg in 1986. It was an offprint of an article that had originally appeared in the *Schmallenberger Heimatblätter. Schmallenberger Heimatblätter* is a local history periodical published by the Scmallenberger Schürengesellschaft (Riflemen's [or "Shooting"] Association). Some issues have individual titles.

13. The literal meaning of *Persilschein* is "Persil certificate," Persil being a popular brand of laundry detergent.

14. The SED is the Sozialistische Einheitspartei Deutschlands (Socialist Unity Party of Germany), the East German Communist Party.

15. The Neue Wache (New Guardhouse) was built during 1816–18 in the form of a Roman fortress according to the plans of the famous architect Karl Friedrich Schinkel, replacing the Königswache (Royal Guardhouse). It was used as a base for the guards of the palace opposite. The interior was converted in 1931 into a war memorial, and in 1960 into a monument to the victims of fascism and militarism.

16. The Treuhandanstalt, or Treuhand for short, was the restructuring agency established in reunited Germany in 1990 to undertake the task of administering and selling off state-owned companies in the former East Germany, that is, of privatizing virtually the whole of the former GDR economy. The Treuhand privatized itself out of existence in December 1994.

AFTERWORD

1. T. W. Adorno, "Was bedeutet: Aufarbeitung der Vergangenheit" (1959), in *Gesammelte Schriften,* v. 10: 2 (Frankfurt am Main: Suhrkamp, 1977), p. 566.

2. Displaying an assortment of documents, images, and paraphernalia, the exhibition, titled *Vernichtungskrieg: Verbrechen der Wehrmacht, 1941–1945 (War of Annihilation: Crimes of the Wehrmacht, 1941–1945),* sought to undercut one of the most cherished myths of the postwar era: that the traditional armed forces had rarely, if ever, contributed to the atrocities committed by the SS or the Einsatzgruppen (mobile killing units). Ordinary German soldiers, it turns out, were often engaged in a war against civilians and prisoners of war (who were often executed rather than imprisoned) that went well beyond the defense against partisan forces that had traditionally been used to justify certain excesses.

3. To date the following biographies have been published: Esther Bejarano, *Man nannte mich Krümel: Eine jüdische Jugend in der Zeit der Verfolgung* 2. Aufl. (Hamburg: Curio, 1991); Flora Neumann, *Erinnern um zu leben: Vor Auschwitz, in Auschwitz, nach Auschwitz* (Hamburg: F. und R. Neumann, 1991); "We Should Squash You Like Cockroaches," in Lore Shelly, ed., *The Union Kommando in Auschwitz: The Auschwitz Munitions Factory Through the Eyes of Its Former Slave Laborers* (Lanham, Md.: University Press of America, 1996), pp. 29–38; Karl Heinz Jahnke, *Sie haben nie aufgegeben: Ettie und Peter Gingold—Widerstand in Frankreich und Deutschland* (Bonn: Pahl-Rugenstein, 1998).

4. Peter Hayes, "I. G. Farben und der I. G. Farben Prozess: Zur Verwicklung eines Großkonzerns in die nationalsozialistischen Vebrechen," in *Jahrbuch zur Geschichte und Wirkung des Holocausts. Auschwitz: Geschichte, Rezeption und Wirking,* published by the Fritz Bauer Institute (1996), p. 99.

5. *Trials of War Criminals before the Nuernberg Military Tribunals under Control Council Law No. 10, Nuernberg October 1946–April 1949* (Washington, D.C.: United States Government Printing Office, 1952), v. 8, pp. 1186–87.

6. Hans Dieter Kreikamp, "Die Entflechtung der I. G. Farbenindustrie A. G. und die Gründung der Nachfolgegesellschaften," in *Vierteljahrshefte für Zeitgeschichte,* v. 25 (1977), pp. 220–51; Karl Heinz Roth, "Einleitung des Bearbeiters," in *OMGUS: Ermittlungen gegen die I. G. Farbenindustrie A. G.—September 1945,* Office of Military Government for Germany, United States, Übersetzt und bearbeitet von der Dokumentationsstelle zur NS-Sozialpolitik Hamburg, edited by Hans Magnus Enzensberger (Nördlingen: Franz Greno, 1986), pp. xiii–lxxii.

7. Cf. Wolfgang Benz, "Der Wollheim-Prozeß: Zwangsarbeit für I. G. Farben in Auschwitz," in Ludolf Herbst and Constantin Goschler, eds., *Wiedergutmachung in der Bundesrepublik Deutschland* (München, 1989), pp. 303–26. We would like to thank Werner Renz of the Fritz Bauer Institute in Frankfurt am Main who helped us gain

access to the files of the Wollheim trial that was held in the third civil court of appeal of the Frankfurt am Main district court (Az. 2/3 O 406/51).

8. Fritz Bauer Institute, Wollheim Trial Collection, Verdict of the Frankfurt am Main District Court of 19 June 1953 (Az. 2/3 O 405/51), p. 17.

9. Ibid., p. 21.

10. Bundesarchiv Koblenz, B 102, No. 60762, Dr. Storkebaum/Dr. Brüstele, Bericht. Betr.: Prozeß des ehemaligen KZ- Häftlings Wollheim gegen die I. G., 5.3.1953. Bl. 3. (Dr. Storkebaum and Dr. Brüstele, Report re: Trial of former concentration camp inmate Wollheim v. I. G., 5 March 1953, p. 3).

11. Benz, "Der Wollheim-Prozeß," p. 308.

12. Ibid., pp. 314ff.

13. Cf. ibid., p. 318, for example, regarding a meeting on 3 December 1954 of the Bundestag committee responsible for questions of indemnification.

14. Bundesarchiv Koblenz, B 102, No. 60762, Reuter/Schmidt, I. G. Farbenindustrie i. L. an Bundeswirtschaftsminister Ludwig Erhard, Betr.: Durchführung der I. G.- Entflechtung und Liquidation und Entschädigung früherer Häftlinge, 14.8.1953. (Reuter and Schmidt, I. G. Farbenindustrie A. G. L. to Federal Economics Minister Ludwig Erhard, re: Implementation of the breakup and liquidation of I. G. and compensation of former [concentration camp] inmates, 14 August 1953).

15. Cf. Benz, "Der Wollheim-Prozeß," p. 318, and Henry Ormond's closing argument before the fifth civil court of appeals of the Frankfurt am Main provincial high court (*Oberlandesgericht*) on 1 March 1955, in *Dachauer Hefte* 2 (1986), p. 151.

16. Gustav Stein (BDI) to State Secretary Globke, 15 March 1956, Bundesarchiv Koblenz, B136, v. 1154, quoted in Benz, "Der Wollheim-Prozeß," p. 322. Stein was referring here to negotiations over the return of German business assets confiscated overseas by the Allies during the Second World War.

17. Before becoming ambassador, Krekeler had completed a training program in chemistry at I. G. Farben. See Hans-Jürgen Döscher, *Verschwörene Gesellschaft: Das Auswärtige Amt unter Adenauer zwischen Neubeginn und Kontinuität* (Berlin: Akademie Verlag, 1995), p. 285.

18. Cf. Benjamin F. Ferencz, "Auschwitz-Überlebende gegen I. G. Farben," in *Lohn des Grauens: Die Entschädigung jüdischer Zwangsarbeiter—ein offenes Kapitel deutscher Nachkriegsgeschichte* (Frankfurt am Main, 1986), pp. 59–97. The author of the article was involved in the negotiations.

19. The law was passed a few months later. It was titled Law on the Public Notification of the Creditors of I. G. Farbenindustrie AG in Liquidation of 27 May 1957 (*Gesetz über den Aufruf der Gläubiger der I. G. Farbenindustrie Aktiengesellschaft in Abwicklung vom 27. Mai 1957*), in *Bundesgesetzblatt* 1957, I, p. 596. The law stipulated that forced laborers had until 31 December 1957 to file claims. After that date their claims were no longer valid.

20. I. G. Farbenindustrie AG in Liquidation, Statement by the I. G. liquidators on the agreement concluded with the Conference on Jewish Material Claims against Germany on 6 February with regard to the settlement of future claims brought by [former] concentration camp inmates allocated during the war to I. G. in the Auschwitz area in need of labor, signed Dr. Brinckmann and Dr. Schmidt, February 1957 (I. G. Farbenindustrie AG Aketiengesellschaft in Abwicklung, Stellungnahme der Liquidatoren der I. G. Farbenindustrie zu dem mit der Conference on Jewish Material Claims against Germany am 6. Februar geschlossenen Abkommen über die Regelung etwaiger Ansprüche

während des Krieges der I. G. im Auschwitz-Bereich zum Arbeitseinsatz zugewiesenen KZ-Häftlinge, gez. Dr. Brinckmann, gez. Dr. Schmidt, Februar 1957).

21. Nikolaus Piper, "I. G. Farben i. A.—Die Erben leben auf: Alte Ansprüche auf Ostvermögen heizen Spekulationen an," in *Die Zeit,* no. 44 (26 October 1990) and Otto Köhler, "Hochstimmung im Schatten der I. G. Auschwitz," in *Die Zeit,* no. 19 (3 March 1991).

❧

Glossary

"Aryanization" (*Arisierung*) Jews had been living under the threat of terror and violence since the beginning of the Nazi regime in 1933. By the time of the Kristallnacht (q.v.) riots on 9–10 November 1938 they had already disposed of approximately 60 percent of their personal property and business assets, in general for much less than their actual worth. They did so either to finance their emigration from Germany or to pay for their subsistence. Since Jews had been prohibited from practicing their professions and suffered from other discriminatory measures, they had no other means of support. The German government tried to use this process of buying out Jewish businesses at a fraction of their market value as a means of filling the state's coffers. In April 1938 the regime decreed that Jews had to disclose their assets and could not use them without first receiving permission from the government. So-called Aryanization specialists and economic advisers to the *Gaue* (administrative districts under the Nazis) worked together with local business associations—the forerunners of today's *Industrie- und Handelskammern* (chambers of commerce)—to secure control of Jewish enterprises. Their task was to determine whether the Jewish businesses that were up for sale should continue to be operated or simply shut down. After Kristallnacht the expropriation was speeded up. With the restrictions imposed on Jews' access to the balances in their bank accounts, the German government effectively increased its wealth by a billion reichsmarks. In addition, insurance companies saved vast sums by refusing to pay for the damages incurred as a result of the November pogrom. Within a few months of Kristallnacht, the Nazis bought out whatever remained of Jewish business assets and real estate. If Jews wanted to escape permanent impoverishment in Germany, they were forced to emigrate.

Association of Critical Shareholders in Germany (Dachverband der Kritischen Aktionärinnen und Aktionäre) The idea for an organization of socially responsible stockholders originated in the United States. In the Federal Republic of Germany, activist investors have joined together in the Association of Critical Shareholders, which advocates a democratic reform of the policies practiced by big business and the major banks. One of the Association's important demands is compensating men and women who were exploited as slave laborers between 1933 and 1945. One means of protest has been to make use of the right of stockholders to speak and offer resolutions at companies' annual meetings and to support their demands through public information campaigns.

Auschwitz During the four years of its existence (1940–45) the Auschwitz concentration camp was the Nazis' largest killing center and German industry's biggest slave labor camp. Jews as well as Sinti and Roma from all over Europe were killed on an assembly-line basis in Auschwitz.

On 27 April 1940 Heinrich Himmler, Reich leader of the SS and chief of the German police (*Reichsführer SS und Chef der Deutschen Polizei*), ordered the SS to build a concentration camp near the Polish town of Auschwitz (Oświęcim), 96.5 kilometers west of the city of Kraków. Initially the camp consisted of Austrian military barracks built in the nineteenth century. In 1944 the so-called base camp, or *Stammlager* (Auschwitz I), encompassed thirty one-story wooden and brick barracks. Block 10 was the place where criminal medical experiments were performed on prisoners; Block 11 was used as a place to punish and torture inmates. In between the two blocks was the infamous "black wall," the execution plaza, where thousands of prisoners were shot to death by the SS.

The first inmates in Auschwitz I were mainly members of the Polish intelligentsia. The occupiers had determined that the Polish intellectual class had to be killed to secure German rule. Himmler first visited Auschwitz on 1 March 1941 and subsequently ordered a massive increase in the size of the camp. The expansion began with the evacuation and deportation of the Polish population in the surrounding villages, which fitted in nicely with the Nazis' policy to Germanize incorporated Polish territory. Beginning in October 1941, 100,000 Soviet prisoners of war were forced to help construct the Birkenau camp, which in January 1942 was designated Auschwitz II. By the spring of 1942, more than 9,000 of the Soviet POWs had died. The Birkenau camp was situated in a closed zone (*Sperrgebiet*) that covered approximately forty square kilometers. It was originally designed to hold 130,000 prisoners, with plans to expand its capacity to 200,000. The first experiments using gas to systematically murder prisoners were conducted on Polish inmates and Soviet POWs. They took place at the base camp during August–September 1941. The so-called "morgue," located to the right of the crematorium, was transformed into the first gas chamber. Starting in January and June 1942, respectively, two cottages at Birkenau (designated as bunkers 1 and 2) that had been transformed into gas chambers were brought into operation. Between March and June 1943, the firm of Topf & Sons in Erfurt helped build the four large crematoria. They were equipped with underground gas chambers disguised as dressing rooms and showers. In this way thousands of people a day were murdered on an assembly-line basis.

A firm called Degesch, the acronym for Deutsche Gesellschaft für Schädlingsbekämpfung (German Company for Pest Control), supplied the poison known as Zyklon-Blausäure (the German word for prussic acid is *Blausäure*), or Zyklon-B, that was used in the gas chambers. The victims suffered an excruciating death by suffocation. Two other companies—Degussa, the acronym for Deutsche Gold- und Silber Scheideanstalt (German Gold and Silver Separating Works), and I. G. Farben—each owned a 42.5 percent interest in Degesch.

Before the Nazis burned the corpses on pyres or incinerated them in the crematoria, they "utilized" them for commercial purposes. Prisoners in the Sonderkommandos (special units of corpse workers in the extermination area) were ordered to remove dental gold from the mouths of prisoners who had died in the gas chambers. The DAW, the acronym for Deutsche Ausrüstungswerke (German Armaments Works), an SS enterprise, produced blankets from the victims' hair.

The transports carrying deportees from all over Europe ended at Auschwitz-Birkenau. The SS forced their victims out of the Reichsbahn (German railway) cattle cars at the *Rampe* (loading platform), which was located next to a railway spur that extended into the camp. There they robbed the Jews of their last remaining possessions before sending them for selection (see "Selection"). The weak, the sick, the elderly, children under the age of fifteen, and pregnant women were driven directly into the gas chambers.

Those who survived the first selection at the time of their arrival in Auschwitz (approximately 15 to 30 percent of the deportees) were registered and received a serial number that was tattooed on their left forearm. After their heads and bodies had been shaved, the prisoners were sent to various other camps.

The base camp (Auschwitz I) held an average of between 15,000 and 18,000 inmates. Birkenau (Auschwitz II), dedicated to the extermination of prisoners in the gas chambers, was constantly being expanded and held some 140,000 inmates in 1943. After August 1942, women in Birkenau were separated from men in a women's camp. In the spring of 1943 a separate "Gypsy camp" was also set up in Birkenau. Between the arrival of the first transport of Sinti and Roma on 26 February 1943 and the evacuation of Auschwitz on 2–3 August 1944, more than 22,000 people in the so-called Gypsy family camp had been murdered.

The third major camp in the vast Auschwitz establishment—Auschwitz III—was opened for business in the spring of 1941 in Monowitz (q.v.).

The exact number of people murdered in Auschwitz is a matter of controversy. First, the perpetrators systematically tried to cover the traces of their crimes. In the summer of 1944, for example, they began burning the lists of deported Jews who arrived in the transports. And second, the fact that an unknown number of deportees were gassed immediately after selection without ever being registered also makes it difficult to determine a precise figure. Numbers appearing in scholarly studies vary from 1.1 million to 1.6 million killed.

The Auschwitz Trial Twenty-one former members of the SS (guards, SS doctors, and orderlies) and one former Auschwitz prisoner were brought to the *Landgericht* (district court) in Frankfurt am Main to stand trial in the proceedings against Robert Karl Ludwig Mulka (SS defendant sentenced to 14 years at hard labor; Lageradjutant [camp adjunct] at Auschwitz—TRANS.) and others (criminal case number 4 Ks 2/63). They were accused of murder and complicity in murder. Charges filed in 1958 against Wilhelm Boger by Hermann Langbein, then secretary of the International Auschwitz Committee, started the move toward holding an "Auschwitz trial." Boger, who was living undisturbed in West Germany, was a former member of the SS who was infamous for the tortures he had devised while he was a guard in the camp. The preliminary proceedings dragged on until Fritz Bauer, the chief public prosecutor of the state of Hesse, overcame the skepticism expressed by members of the West German judiciary about actually bringing the matter to trial. In 1963, five years after Langbein had filed charges, the actual trial of the Auschwitz defendants began in Frankfurt am Main.

The scale of the pretrial investigation, the number of witnesses examined (365), and the length of the trial itself (183 days), which lasted until August 1965, were without precedent in West German legal history. To make room for interested members of the public, the court held its first sessions in the main assembly hall of Frankfurt's historic old town hall and then moved in 1964 to the Haus Gallus. Something quite new in a German trial was the visit in December 1964 by the judge, assistants of the court, prosecutors, and defense attorneys to the site of the former extermination camp. The Polish government had given its permission for members of the court to come to Poland even before the Polish People's Republic had established diplomatic relations with the Federal Republic of Germany.

As a result of the trial, Auschwitz and the crimes committed there became, for the first time, a major issue in West German legal circles and a topic of discussion among members of the broader public. Testimony by witnesses and the findings of experts as well as a wealth of documents read aloud during the proceedings gave people an insight into the origin, structure, and operation of industrialized mass murder in Auschwitz.

The depressing testimony by surviving prisoners from a number of countries not only helped clarify the circumstances of the case and the individual responsibility of the various defendants, it also painted a picture of everyday "life" and the condition of prisoners inside the death camp. The testimony of the survivors stood in stark contrast to that of the defendants, who showed no remorse and maintained throughout the trial that they could not remember anything. The summations began in May 1965, and the judge pronounced sentences on 19–20 August 1965. They fell far short of what the prosecution had asked for. Two of the defendants who had been excused from appearing at the trial for reasons of health were never brought to justice. Three of the defendants were acquitted. Eleven were given sentences ranging from three to fourteen years, and six were sentenced to life in prison.

Block chief (*Blockälteste*) The block chief was a prisoner-functionary appointed by the SS. He was responsible to the SS Blockführer for en-suring discipline and cleanliness in his block. He wore the number of his block on the left sleeve of his coat as a sign of his rank. He was also allowed to have a specially partitioned-off area in a barrack.

Blockführer (block leader) The Blockführer was a member of the SS who supervised one or more blocks. He had virtually unlimited power over the prisoners, their physical and mental well-being, and their lives. The Blockführers were permitted to order corporal pun-ishment and to torture and even kill prisoners.

Classifications The SS visibly marked different classes of prisoners in the concentration and extermination camps and deliberately treated them unequally as a means to divide them from one another and solid-ify their own power. Despite the fact that the SS sometimes managed the camps in an arbitrary and inconsistent fashion, a system of classifi-cation nevertheless emerged. Prisoners were made to wear badges. Col-ored triangles were sewn onto the prisoners' uniforms on the left side of the chest and the right trouser leg. Political prisoners got a red badge, "criminal" prisoners a green badge. Jehovah's Witnesses were required to wear a violet triangle, *Asoziale* (antisocial elements) a black triangle. The pink triangle was introduced for homosexuals and the brown for Gypsies. Jews were required to wear a yellow triangle under their other insignia, so creating a six-pointed star. Foreigners had the beginning letter of their nationality inscribed on their triangle: P for Polish, F for French, and so on. In the Auschwitz death camp, prisoners also had an identification number tattooed on their left forearm.

Death march "Death march," a term coined by concentration camp inmates, referred to periods of time when Jewish and other prisoners were forced to march through the countryside from one place to an-other, guarded by a contingent of Germans, sometimes supplemented by non-German auxiliaries. During the marches the guards brutally mistreated prisoners and murdered many of them. The Nazis eu-phemistically called the death marches "evacuations."

The first death march organized by the SS took place in Poland, in mid-January 1940. Eight hundred Jewish prisoners of war from the Polish army were escorted by a troop of mounted SS men and marched in bitter cold a distance of approximately a hundred kilometers. Only a few dozen survived to reach their destination.

Following the German invasion of the Soviet Union in the summer of 1941, hundreds of thousands of Soviet prisoners of war were moved along the highways of occupied Ukraine and Belorussia. They were transferred from one camp to another and murdered in their masses en route or at prearranged slaughter sites. At roughly the same time, in July and August 1941, tens of thousands of Jews were also marched along the roads of the occupied rear areas, where their German and other escorts shot thousands upon thousands of them to death.

The dismantling of the concentration camps began in the summer of 1944, during the great Red Army offensive in the east and the Allied landings in the west. The first camps to be evacuated were those closest to the front. The SS deported the prisoners to areas that were still under German control. The marches lasted as long as a month and often covered distances of several hundred kilometers. Guards shot prisoners who could not continue the march. This often amounted to entire columns of marchers. In the last two months of the Third Reich's existence, the evacuation of the camps was generally a combined operation: the prisoners made their way partly on foot and partly by train. The train trip was no less harsh or cruel than the foot march; the prisoners suffered from intolerably foul air in the cars, which held an average of seventy persons each, and from lack of food and water. During the winter of 1944–45 hundreds froze to death in the trains. The last camp from which prisoners were sent on a death march was at Reichenau, in the Sudetic Mountains. This took place on 7 May 1945, one day before Germany surrendered to the Allies.

The precise number of people who died during these marches is unknown. It is estimated that of the 750,000 concentration camp inmates who were forced on marches, somewhere between 250,000 and 375,000 were murdered. The brutal treatment of prisoners and the killings by their escorts often took place on the highways in full view of the local population.

Gestapo After 1933 the Nazis continued to use the former political police of the various German states. They renamed them Secret State Police (Geheime Staatspolizei), soon abbreviated as Gestapo. The most powerful weapon the Gestapo had at its disposal to repress anti-Fascists and other groups defined as enemies of the Nazi regime was "protective custody" (*Schutzhaft*). Not subject to any judicial restraints, the Gestapo used protective custody to arrest and torture tens of thousands of people, that is, to send them to prison or spirit them away to a concentration or labor camp. In June 1936 Heinrich Himmler became chief of all German police under the title Reichsführer SS und Chef der Deutschen Polizei. He immediately centralized and expanded the police apparatus and divided it into two branches. First, there was the plainclothes Security Police, or Sipo (Sicherheitspolizei), which was made up of the Criminal Police, or Kripo (Kriminalpolizei), and the Gestapo, including the Border Police (Grenzpolizei). This division came under Reinhard Heydrich. Second was the uniformed Order Police, or Orpo (Ordnungspolizei), under Kurt Daluege, which consisted of the State Police, or Schupo (Schutzpolizei), and the Gendarmerie. The Security Service, or SD (Sicherheitsdienst), of the SS under Heydrich was the Nazi Party's domestic and foreign intelligence branch. In 1939 Himmler issued an order in pursuance of which the SD and the Hauptamt Sicherheitspolizei (Main Office Security Police) were amalgamated into the Reich Security Main Office, or RSHA (Reichssicherheitshauptamt). During the war the Gestapo placed its officials at the disposal of the Einsatzgruppen of the SS, mobile killing units in the occupied territories that moved closely on the heels of the advancing German armies. In addition, Gestapo officials were responsible for deporting Jews to the death camps (see "Transports"). In 1944 the Gestapo had thirty thousand members. The International Military Tribunal in Nuremberg declared the Gestapo a criminal organization.

Hanukkah (Hebrew, "dedication") A Jewish festival celebrated in December commemorating the rededication of the Temple in Jerusalem under Judas Maccabaeus in 165 B.C.E.. The central act of the celebration is the kindling of lights in an eight-branched candelabrum. On each successive night another candle is added, which is why it is also called the Festival of Lights.

Hitler Youth Founded in 1926, the Hitler Youth was the Nazi Party's organization of young people. Even before Hitler became chancellor in 1933, the Nazis used it as an instrument in their campaign of violence against those who opposed them. After the National Socialists came to power in 1933 they outlawed and crushed their opponents' youth organizations, especially those associated with the trade union and labor movements. The Nazis forcibly amalgamated the remaining youth organizations into the Reich Committee of Youth

Associations (Reichsausschuß deutscher Jugendverbände). The Hitler Youth was subdivided by age: the *Jungvolk* (ten-to-fourteen-year-old boys), the *Jungmädel* (ten-to-fourteen-year-old girls), the League of German Girls, or *Bund Deutscher Mädel* (fifteen-to-eighteen-year-old girls), and the actual Hitler Youth (fifteen-to-eighteen-year-old boys). Service in the Hitler Youth was meant to inculcate a "martial spirit" in the young. Besides excursions and rituals, many of the organization's activities revolved around sports and ideological "instruction" (especially in the history of the Nazi Party and "racial anthropology"). The Hitler Youth's activities were mainly designed to prepare boys for military service by marching and drilling them, taking them to visit military installations, and giving them basic infantry training. In 1939 membership in the Hitler Youth became obligatory for all "Aryan" young people. During the war, members of the Hitler Youth had jobs in the wartime economy and served as flak helpers (*Flakhelfers*), replacing antiaircraft soldiers needed at the front, and as auxiliary air raid wardens.

Israel and **Sara** A decree issued by the Interior Ministry on 18 August 1939 stipulated that as of 1 January 1939 all Jewish men and Jewish women residing within the German sphere of influence were to have Jewish first names (cf. *Reichsgesetzblatt* I, 1044 [1939]). A list of approved names drawn up by Ministerialrat (civil service expert) Hans Globke was attached to the decree. Jewish men whose names did not appear on the approved list had to add to their regular first name the middle name Israel, and Jewish women the name Sara. The name changes and new names had to be recorded on birth and marriage certificates by the local Order Police. Henceforth the new designations also had to appear in court records and all official correspondence dealing with individually named Jews.

Kapos Kapos were prisoners appointed by the SS to supervise work Kommandos or to oversee various services inside the camp (see "Prisoner-functionaries"). Kapos were subordinate to an SS Kommando leader (*Kommandoführer*) and were made responsible for filling compulsory production quotas. They were encouraged, under threat of punishment, to carry out their tasks with military discipline and utmost brutality. A number of Kapos became submissive instruments of their SS masters, but there were also Kapos who tried to avoid employing terror and violence against their fellow prisoners and used their power to help inmates survive and allow the Resistance to operate inside the camp. The derivation of the term *Kapo* is in dispute. It may come from the Italian word *capo* (chief, head) or it may be an acronym for *Kameradschaftspolizei* (comradeship police).

Kristallnacht (*Reichskristallnacht*, Crystal Night, Night of Broken Glass, and Night of Shattered Glass) The pogrom euphemistically known as Kristallnacht took place on 9 November 1938. The name comes from *Kristallglas* (beveled plate glass) and refers to the broken windows of Jewish stores. The riots came as the culmination of efforts to expel Polish Jews living and working in Germany. The catalytic development was the deportation of about seventeen thousand Polish Jews who were driven into a no-man's-land between the two countries on 28 October 1938, following a ploy of the Polish government intended to deprive Polish Jews of the right of return from countries under German rule. The greatest number of the deportees was left stranded near the border for days. In this group were the parents of Herschel Grynszpan, a seventeen-year-old Polish Jew who had grown up in Germany. News of their plight and the persecution of Jews in Germany generally drove the desperate youth to seek revenge. On 7 November he shot Ernst vom Rath, a minor German Foreign Office official, in the German embassy in Paris. Two days later vom Rath died of his wounds. The Nazis seized the opportunity to conduct a pogrom and officially present it as a spontaneous outburst provoked by the assassination of vom Rath. The same evening at a meeting of Nazi leaders in Munich, Propaganda Minister Joseph Goebbels, with Hitler's consent, harangued the party veterans and hinted that this was the hour for action against the Jews. The leaders of the SA immediately phoned their subordinates and ordered them to send out their brigades to demolish Jewish-owned stores and systematically burn down all the synagogues in the country. And Gestapo headquarters in Berlin sent a telex to its regional offices "not to interfere with the actions against Jews, especially not against their synagogues." In addition, the chief of the SS and the police ordered his forces to make preparations for "the arrest of some 20,000 to 30,000 Jews within the Reich." Members of the SA and the Nazi Party as well as members of the Hitler Youth and other Nazi organizations helped set fire to synagogues, ransacked approximately 7,500 businesses, and destroyed innumerable private residences. Segments of the general populace also took part in the riots and used the occasion to loot destroyed stores. Fire departments had been ordered not to fight fires unless flames threatened to spread to nearby buildings not owned by Jews. The police refused to intervene unless the looting got totally out of control. According to official figures, at least 91 people were murdered. However, the actual number of victims who perished during the pogrom or were driven to suicide has been estimated at between 2,000 and 2,500. Approximately 30,000 men and boys were arrested and imprisoned in the concentration camps of Buchenwald, Dachau, and Sachsenhausen, where many of them died as a result of physical and mental abuse. Most of those who had been imprisoned were forced to waive the rights to their possessions, most of which were not returned until they had paid the taxes imposed on Jews who were emigrating.

Kristallnacht was a turning point. The expulsion of the Jews to other countries was to be speeded up and the last phase of Aryanization (q.v.) was to begin. Germany was to become *judenfrei* (free of Jews). In addition, the pogrom's very violence served to prepare the non-Jewish population for the war the Nazis had already decided to instigate.

Labor Deployment (*Arbeitseinsatz*) Even before the pogrom that was conducted across Germany and Austria on 9–10 November 1938 (see *"Kristallnacht"*), the Nazis were busy drafting laws and decrees designed to further exclude Jews from participation in German society and above all to isolate them from non-Jewish Germans. Upon the recommendation of the Reich Institute for Employment and Unemployment Relief (Reichsanstalt für Arbeitsvermittlung und Arbeitslosenfürsorge), unemployed Jews were to be forced into the lowest-paying jobs, regardless of the occupations for which they had been trained or the most recent occupation in which they had been engaged. By the end of 1939, towns and municipalities as well as privately owned companies had conscripted twenty thousand Jewish men and women to work in segregated labor brigades (*Arbeitskolonnen*), chiefly on construction and reclamation projects and in garbage collection. In the spring of 1940 the Germans extended this so-called Separate Labor Deployment (Geschlossener Arbeitseinsatz) to include German Jews who were fit for work but unsupported by public funds. Even armaments firms employed Jewish men and women as forced laborers, putting them in partitioned-off production areas or ensuring their isolation from non-Jewish workers by the use of special badges. By the turn of the year 1940–41, the Nazis had conscripted 40,000 German Jews as part of *Geschlossener Arbeitseinsatz* to work in cities, the building and construction industry, and the armaments industry. In the summer of 1941 the vocational education and retraining camps operated by the Reich Association of Jews in Germany (Reichsvereinigung der Juden in Deutschland) were either shut down or reorganized within the framework of the forced labor system. By the end of July 1941 between 51,000 and 53,000 German Jewish men and women were employed as forced laborers, that is, up to 90 percent of able-bodied Jews had been conscripted as part of *Geschlossener Arbeitseinsatz*. To date, researchers have been able to document the existence of some 125 labor and residential camps that were established in connection with the forced-labor system in Germany.

Mittelbau-Dora The building of a camp near Nordhausen began a few days after intensive bombings by the Allied air forces on 17–18 August 1943 had destroyed the Peenemünde Research Center, where antiaircraft gunsights were produced and the long-range V-2 rocket was developed; it was also the final test site for live firings of the completed rockets. Reich Minister for Munitions and War Production Albert Speer and Reichsführer SS Heinrich Himmler immediately decided to relocate the Peenemünde experimentation facility and production works. They settled on Kohnstein—a hill six kilometers from Nordhausen—as the site to build tunnels for rocket and weapons production. The companies involved in the project formed a new firm, the Mittelwerk. The commandant of the Mittelbau-Dora subcamp was made a member of the firm's board of directors and given the title *Arbeitsdirektor* (work director). By the end of 1943 the SS had brought approximately seventeen thousand prisoners from the Buchenwald concentration camp to help complete the tunnel system. Twenty-five percent of these prisoners died building the tunnel factories. The prisoners were forced to work underground around the clock in shifts. Some of them were housed in the tunnels, where they lived in damp, dusty rooms without ventilation or light. Because of the high mortality rate, the Nazis built a crematorium on the hillside in January 1944. During that same year, a number of armaments firms moved their production facilities to the Mittelbau complex. Dora, the cover name for the concentration camp established in the Hartz Mountains, was originally founded as a subcamp of Buchenwald in September 1943. In October 1944 the Buchenwald subcamp was combined with the Dora base camp, the large subcamps at Ellrich and Harzungen, and more than thirty other smaller subcamps and external work Kommandos (*Außenkommandos*) to become an independent concentration camp. It was organized under the name Mittelbau. The number of inmates in the Mittelbau concentration camp rose from approximately 12,500 at the end of the construction phase in late March 1944 to some 45,000 prisoners by the end of December 1944.

About a hundred prisoners a day died as a result of the inhuman working conditions and the arbitrary cruelty of the SS. In January 1945 the SS converted the former *Boelke Kaserne* (barracks) at Nordhausen into a "recuperation" camp, whose real purpose was the slow but sure extermination of prisoners who were no longer able to work. Between January and March 1945, about eighteen thousand prisoners arrived in Mittelbau-Dora. The SS had marched them from Auschwitz, Groß Rosen, and other camps with an eye to using them as forced laborers west of the advancing Red Army. At the beginning of April 1945, the Nazis evacuated Dora and its subcamps. It is likely that they held forty thousand inmates at the time. Except for a small group of prisoners with technical skills who were transported to Ebensee in Austria to continue building rockets, prisoners were forced to march in the direction of Sachsenhausen or Belsen. When the Americans liberated Nordhausen on 11 April 1945 they found 680 prisoners who had been left behind. The few survivors of the death marches were liberated in early May in the area around Mecklenburg northwest of the Hartz Mountains and in Bergen-Belsen.

Monowitz (Auschwitz III) Auschwitz III was established as a result of Buna chemical plant no. 4 that I. G. Farben had begun to build in the spring of 1941. The factory was classified as "critical for the war effort."

As early as November 1939, Farben had developed plans for building a huge chemical complex in Upper Silesia. In the fall of 1940 the Farben leadership intensified its search for a site in which to locate its synthetic-rubber and petroleum works. The management's intention was to exploit the Wehrmacht's increased need for *Buna* (synthetic rubber), caused by the war, to further its own objectives: developing new technologies, expanding investments, and boosting profits. Farben managers brought their construction plans into line with the racist policy of Germanization espoused by the Reich Commissioner for the Consolidation of the German Nation (Reichskommissar für die Festigung deutschen Volkstums), Heinrich Himmler. I. G. Farben employees moved into the houses and apartments of deported Jews and Poles. Farbenindustrie acquired the land of the evicted owners at give-away prices. The Main Trustee Office East (Haupttreuhandstelle Ost) assured the company a supply of cheap energy as a result of the government-organized robbery of the Upper Silesian coal mines. There was an additional factor that was of critical importance in Farben's choice of Auschwitz as the site for its chemical complex. The SS had promised before construction had begun that the firm would be able to employ thousands of prisoners from the nearby concentration camp as slave laborers.

When construction started in April 1941 the first prisoner work Kommandos were forced to march seven kilometers under SS guard from the Auschwitz base camp to the building site and back again. But I. G. Farben wanted to employ an even larger number of prisoners and increase their output by eliminating the march back and forth, so the company paid to set up its own concentration camp on the grounds of the Buna works. In order to free up space for the facility, Farben forcibly resettled the inhabitants of the village of Monowitz. In late October 1942 the first prisoners were transferred to the Monowitz concentration camp. By the summer of 1944 their numbers had grown to more than ten thousand.

From an organizational point of view, the camp at Monowitz evolved into a satellite camp of Auschwitz and became known as Auschwitz III. There were more than forty subcamps at Monowitz, all of which came under the command of SS Hauptstürmführer (Captain) Heinrich Schwarz. In many of the subcamps I. G. Farben's subsidiary companies exploited prisoner labor in the coal mines of Upper Silesia. The average life expectancy in the mines was one to two months, even less than that at Monowitz, where prisoners averaged between three and four months.

It is estimated that thirty thousand prisoners were murdered at Monowitz alone. Many died as a result of industrial accidents caused by the absence of any safety provisions for workers. The most common cause of death, however, was emaciation resulting from total physical exhaustion, permanent malnutrition, and untreated illnesses. When

Farben representatives were dissatisfied with the low output of prisoners or their inability to perform due to sickness or disability, they would see to it that the SS selected them for extermination in Birkenau.

Muselmann *Muselmann* (literally, "Muslim"; plural *Muselmänner*) was Auschwitz jargon for an inmate who was physically and psychologically destroyed by hunger, disease, or simply the brutality of camp life. Owing to the harsh working conditions in the camp and the complete lack of adequate nutrition, many inmates became living skeletons, easily susceptible to disease. They had a dull and expressionless look in their eyes and were indifferent to their surroundings and their fate. *Muselmänner* stood at the very bottom of the camp hierarchy. A person who had reached the *Muselmann* stage had no chance of survival. The origin of the term has not been established; some have attributed it to a certain similarity between a concentration camp *Muselmann* and a Muslim prostrating himself in prayer.

Nuremberg Laws On the occasion of the 1935 Nazi Party rally in the city of Nuremberg, Hitler ordered that a decree be written to define what was actually meant by "Jew." Since the subsequent Reich Citizenship Law (Reichsbürgergesetz) and the Law for the Protection of German Blood and German Honor (Gesetz zum Schutze des deutschen Blutes und der deutschen Ehre) came into force at the end of the rally, on 15 September 1935, they are referred to as the Nuremberg Laws. To the existing concept of citizenship, the Reich Citizenship Law added that of "citizen of the Reich" (*Reichsbürger*). In the words of the law, the only persons to enjoy full political rights ("*der alleinige Träger vollen politischen Rechte*") were those of "German or related blood . . . who demonstrate by [their] behavior that [they] are willing and able to loyally serve the German Reich." The Law for the Protection of German Blood and German Honor made relationships between Jews and non-Jews punishable by law. It prohibited marriages and extramarital intercourse between Jews and citizens of "German or related blood." It also made it easier for "mixed" couples to divorce and to annul "mixed" marriages. It was sufficient for someone to accuse someone else of having "defiled the [Aryan] race" (*Rassenschande*) to have the latter—Jew or non-Jew—brought before a special court and sentenced to imprisonment in a concentration camp. The employment in Jewish households of female citizens of "German or related blood" under the age of forty-five was also forbidden. On

14 November 1935 the Interior Ministry issued its First Regulation to the Reich Citizenship Law defining who was a Jew. This provided the basis for subsequent measures that ultimately led to the total disenfranchisement of Jewish Germans, excluding them from participation in German society and depriving them of their livelihoods. On 26 November 1935 the Interior Ministry issued a Second Regulation expanding the group of those affected by the Law for the Protection of German Blood. The regulation made "marriages of persons of German blood with Gypsies, Negroes and their bastards" punishable by law.

Ortsbauernführer (local farmers' leader) The Ortsbauernführer was a functionary of the Reich Food Estate (Reichsnährstand), a monopoly organization established by law on 13 September 1933 that encompassed all persons and businesses involved in agricultural production (including the cultivation, processing, and marketing of farm products) and absorbed all the agricultural-interest organizations that had been disbanded by the Nazis. Membership was obligatory. As a professional organization, the Reich Food Estate was subject to the so-called Leadership Principle (*Führerprinzip*), whereby individual Nazis were placed above bureaucratic structures as the final authority. As an organ of the state, it came under the Reich Farmers' Leader and Reich Minister for Food and Agriculture (Reichsbauernführer und Reichsminister für Ernährung und Landwirtschaft). The Reich Food Estate was not legally dissolved until 1949.

Ortsgruppenleiter of the NSDAP (local group leader of the Nazi Party) The NSDAP was strictly organized, down to the smallest regional unit. Forty to sixty households constituted a *Block,* or "street block," the smallest regional administrative unit. Four to eight blocks (*Blöcke*) formed a cell (*Zell*), and three to five cells a "local group" (*Ortsgruppe*), whose head, the Ortsgruppenleiter, wielded political power and was therefore accorded a certain degree of authority. Above the group leaders, in ascending order, were the district leaders (*Kreisleiter*), the administrative region leaders (*Gauleiter*), the eighteen Reich leaders (*Reichsleiter*), and the "Führer" and Reich leader Adolf Hitler. The most important task of the political leaders was to keep tabs on the state of mind of the people. To accomplish this task they worked hand in hand with the Gestapo and the Security Service (Sicherheitsdienst, or SD). In 1946 the International Military Tribunal in Nuremberg classified the entire corps of the NSDAP's political leadership—a total of approximately 700,000 party leaders—as a criminal organization.

Prisoner-functionaries (*Funktionshäftlinge*) Prisoner-functionaries were camp inmates chosen by the SS to carry out specific tasks. They included senior camp prisoners (*Lagerältesten*), block chiefs (*Blockältesten*), camp scribes or clerks (*Lagerschreibers*), Kapos, prisoner-physicians, and so on. They wore corresponding armbands to distinguish them. The status conferred on prisoner-functionaries increased their chances of survival. They received better accommodations, clothing, and food and were exempted from performing heavy physical labor. They were responsible to the SS for ensuring that the camp administration ran smoothly and in exchange they were granted wide-ranging, often unlimited power over subordinate prisoners. They were permitted to mete out punishments and even to kill. The larger the camp, the more the SS depended on prisoner participation in administration and the more opportunities the prisoner-functionaries had to act on behalf of their fellow inmates. The question of which particular prisoner-functionaries carried out these functions and how they did so was of critical importance in creating an environment in which the Resistance movement could survive and grow.

The SS preferred to use non-Jewish German prisoners as prisoner-functionaries, especially so-called professional criminals, or "greens." Although not all greens allowed themselves to become tools of the SS—just as not all political prisoners ("reds"; see "Classifications") performed their functions for the benefit of other prisoners—inmates feared camps in which most of the prisoner-functionaries were greens. In many concentration camps a fierce power struggle developed between reds and greens over who was to occupy influential positions in the camp hierarchy. Only in rare instances did Jewish inmates become prisoner-functionaries.

Resistance at Auschwitz Given the conditions that existed in an extermination camp, the first aim of the Resistance movement was to protect prisoners' lives. In contrast to individual forms of resistance—such as helping individual fellow inmates—the organized form encompassed every effort and action that was directed against the SS's claim to absolute power and against any further deterioration in living conditions generally. The political makeup of the Resistance groups shifted as the composition of the prisoner population changed.

Initially the Poles constituted the dominant Resistance group at Auschwitz. This changed, however, as more and more of the prisoners who were deported to Auschwitz came from the other occupied countries of Europe. Experienced cadres from the labor movements of various countries, together with representatives of organizations associated with the Jewish labor movement and Jewish middle-class opposition parties, formed the nucleus of the illegal cells. Despite communication problems due to linguistic differences and the national and anti-Semitic prejudices that emerged from time to time, the cells successfully linked up to form a camp-wide organization.

Among the Resistance movement's most urgent tasks was the procurement of additional food, medicine, and clothing. Since even the slightest act of resistance involved the danger of being discovered, tortured, and executed, protecting the movement from infiltration by informants of the Political Department (Politische Abeteilung), as the camp Gestapo was known, and exposing informants were of paramount importance.

The Resistance documented the crimes committed at Auschwitz. At great peril to themselves, escapees and couriers smuggled photographs, maps of the camp, building plans, reports (for example, copies of transport lists, lists containing the names of prisoners who had been shot to death), and letters to underground Resistance groups outside the camp.

Prisoners who were employed as forced laborers by Krupp, Siemens, the Weichsel-Union works, or I. G. Farben managed to disrupt wartime production by sabotaging raw materials, equipment, production lines, and finished products.

Of the more than 800 attempts to escape from Auschwitz, only 144 were ultimately successful. For those escapees who did not speak Polish, there was the problem of communication. And Jewish prisoners who managed to flee had the additional burden of coping with the anti-Semitism that was widespread among the Polish populace. If an escaped prisoner did not succeed in making contact with Resistance fighters or partisan bands soon after fleeing the camp, his or her chances of survival diminished rapidly.

The Auschwitz Battle Group (Kampfgruppe Auschwitz) was founded in 1943 at the initiative of Austrian prisoners. Its aim was armed resistance inside the camp. Made up of members from a number of different countries, the Group helped lay the groundwork for the revolt of the Sonderkommando, which was the culmination of the Resistance's armed struggle. The Sonderkommando was a special unit of Jewish prisoners who were forced, under SS guard, to work cremating the corpses of the murder victims. Hearing that they themselves were about to be killed, the members of the unit decided in October 1944 to rise up against their SS masters. On 7 October some three hundred prisoners attacked startled SS men with axes, hammers, stones, several revolvers, and a light machine gun. They managed to set crematorium no. 4 on fire and set off some homemade explosive devices. Jewish women employed in the nearby Weichsel-Union metal works had stolen incendiary chemicals from the factory and smuggled them to the Sonderkommando in Birkenau. During the ensuing encounters with the SS guards, a number of prisoners managed to escape. When the SS finally intercepted them, the prisoners barricaded themselves in a barn and fought back. The SS set the barn on fire and burned some 250 prisoners alive. The same evening, the survivors of the uprising were shot to death. Crematorium no. 4 could never again be used to gas prisoners, thereby slowing down the process of extermination.

Selection The term coined by Darwin to describe his theory of biological evolution was "natural selection." The social Darwinists changed its meaning, applying Darwin's idea of the "struggle for life" in nature to human society and calling for the *Selection* of the "best" human beings. The Nazis integrated social Darwinism into their racial ideology. In Auschwitz selection referred to the separation, mainly by SS doctors, of new arrivals into those who were "still fit for work" (and would be allowed to live for a limited period of time) and those who were to be immediately murdered.

Shabbat *Shabbat,* the Jewish Sabbath, comes from the Hebrew word for "rest" or "cessation." Shabbat is observed from sunset Friday until sunset Saturday. The reason for the observance, according to the Torah, is that God made the world in six days, and rested on the seventh day. Shabbat is to be spent in solemn rest and religious contemplation. Traditionally Shabbat begins at home with prayers, the lighting of candles, and the recitation of blessings over the Sabbath repast. The following day, passages from the Torah are read during services held in the synagogue.

SS Abbreviation of *Schutzstaffel* (protective echelon), the black-uniformed elite corps of the Nazi Party. Founded by Adolf Hitler in

April 1925 as a small personal bodyguard, the SS grew with the success of the Nazi movement and, gathering immense police and military powers, became virtually a state within the state.

From 1929 until its dissolution in 1945, the SS was headed by Heinrich Himmler, the Reichsführer SS (Reich leader of the SS), who built up the SS from fewer than 300 members to more than 50,000 by the time the Nazis came to power in 1933.

When Hitler, with SS help, liquidated the SA high command in 1934 and reduced the SA to political impotence, the SS became an independent group responsible, via Himmler, to Hitler alone. Between 1934 and 1936, Hitler and his chief adjunct, Reinhard Heydrich, consolidated SS strength by gaining control of all of Germany's police forces and expanding their organization's responsibilities and activities. This included the duty of administering the concentration camps.

At the same time special military SS units were trained and equipped along the lines of a regular army. By 1939 the SS, now numbering 250,000 men, had become a huge labyrinthine bureaucracy, divided mainly into two groups: the Allgemeine SS (General SS) and the Waffen SS (Armed SS).

Himmler succeeded in transforming the SS into a mass army on which was to rest the ultimate exercise of Nazi power. And with Hitler's agreement he also formed an SS economic empire that controlled vast business and manufacturing enterprises.

The International Military Tribunal in Nuremberg in 1946 found the SS guilty of persecuting and exterminating Jews, of brutalities and killings in concentration camps, of excesses in the administration of occupied territories, of administration of the slave labor program, and of mistreatment of prisoners of war.

Theresienstadt (Czech: "Terezín") The town of Terezín in northwestern Czechoslovakia had a population of less than 7,000 before World War II. In November 1941 the SS began expelling the non-Jewish inhabitants from the town, transforming it into a transient concentration camp, and officially labeling it a ghetto. After the summer of 1942 the more than 75,000 Czech and Slovak Jews who had been deported to Theresienstadt were followed by transports with a total of 42,000 German, 15,000 Austrian, 5,000 Dutch, and 500 Danish Jews. Many of the victims of these "old people's transports" hoped that this "transfer of residence" to the "community ghetto" of Theresienstadt, as it was called, would exempt them from deportation to the east. However, for 88,000 out of the 141,000 Jewish men and women who were deported to Theresienstadt, it was merely a stopover on the way to the ghettos and extermination camps farther east. And from there only 3,500 ever returned alive; 35,500 out of the 141,000 deportees died in Theresienstadt itself. A Nazi propaganda film titled *The Führer Presents the Jews with a City* (*Der Führer schenkt den Juden eine Stadt*) has perpetuated the myth of the "model ghetto" down to the present day. The Germans shot the film in the wake of a visit to the ghetto by an International Red Cross investigation committee. In preparation for the visit, the Nazis had deported more prisoners than usual to Auschwitz so as to reduce the ghetto population of its congestion and make it look more presentable.

Transports (also referred to as Deportations from the Reich) After Germany's invasion of the Soviet Union on 22 June 1941, the plans for deporting German Jews developed by the Reich Security Main Office (Reichsicherheitshauptamt, or RSHA) under Reinhard Heydrich were put into action. The nature of the deportations changed fundamentally from their prewar function. They were no longer a means to expel Jews from Germany; rather, they were now designed to facilitate their extermination. On 31 July 1941 Reichsmarschall Hermann Göring had given Heydrich the order to organize "a complete solution of the Jewish question in the German sphere of influence in Europe." When Heydrich presented his plans for the "final solution" to representatives of the other Reich ministries at a conference held in the Berlin suburb of Wannsee on 31 January 1942, the mass deportations of Austrian and German Jews had already begun. From the middle of October to the beginning of November 1941, fifteen deportation trains departed from the cities of Vienna, Berlin, Cologne, Düsseldorf, Hamburg, and Frankfurt, as well as the country of Luxembourg. Their destination, as determined by the RSHA, was the Litzmannstadt (Łódź) ghetto in occupied Poland. (The Germans had renamed the city of Łódź in honor of the German general who captured the city from the Russians during the First World War.) It is assumed that except for a few dozen survivors, most of the fourteen thousand deportees were murdered in the Kulmhof (Chełmno) extermination camp, the construction of which had begun in December 1941.

"Labor deployment," a euphemism for various forms of forced labor in the Third Reich, did not automatically exempt Jews from being deported, especially at the beginning of the mass deportations in 1941–42. The question of whether a Jewish forced laborer was to be deported or—temporarily—deferred from deportation depended on the interplay of forces at the time and the way in which the various armaments inspectors (*Rüstungsinspektoren*), labor offices, and business enterprises represented their interests to Gestapo officials. Employees of the Jewish communities who dealt with the Gestapo officials on a daily basis and on whose cooperation the Gestapo depended in carrying out the deportations rarely succeeded in obtaining deferments for either individuals or groups.

The 20,000 German Jews deported from major metropolitan areas in Germany were murdered in Minsk, Kovno (Kaunas), and Riga; the deportations from Germany's big cities continued until January 1942. The 1,350 Jews deported from Dortmund on 25 January 1942 also ended up in Riga. A second deportation train transported 1,200 Westphalian Jews from Dortmund to Zamość near Lublin on 27 April 1942. It is presumed that they were murdered at the killing centers in Sobibór and Bełzec. The deportations to Theresienstadt began in May 1942. In 1942 the Auschwitz-Birkenau extermination center became the destination for most of the deportations from Germany. A transport from Dortmund in July 1942 included 1,000 Jews from the district of Arnsberg. The so-called factory action, or roundup, of February 1943, of which the labor offices had been informed in December 1942, marked the end of the mass deportations of German Jews to the east. During the roundup the Gestapo raided businesses and residences or simply arrested their victims on the street.

More than 130,000 Jews deported from Germany were killed in the ghettos and extermination camps. The deportations of German Jews from the cities and towns of the Reich were carried out in public. After the deportations, employers, factory managers, landlords, bank clerks, shipping agents, secondhand dealers, and a bevy of government officials and municipal employees contacted the tax authorities to settle any outstanding debts. Or they simply made use of what remained of the deportees' assets. Clearly, they knew that the Jews would not be coming back.

Waffen SS On 17 August 1938, Hitler declared that in order to fulfill special domestic tasks of a political nature certain SS units, including the Totenkopfverbände (Death's Head Units) posted as guards at concentration camps, were to be armed, trained, and organized as military units, outside the structure of both the army and the police. Originally called the SS Verfügungstruppe (SS Special Service Troops at the personal disposal of the Führer), they became known as the Waffen SS (Armed SS) after the outbreak of war in 1939. Beginning with a force of approximately eighteen thousand men in 1939, the Waffen SS continued to grow in strength throughout the war years until by December 1944 it had more than thirty divisions in the field and numbered approximately six hundred thousand men. The men of the Waffen SS were notorious for their cruelty toward the civilian population.

Wehrmacht The German armed forces (literally, "defense force"). The term was sometimes used as though synonymous with "German army," but it referred to the navy and Luftwaffe as well.

Yom Kippur (Day of Atonement) A solemn Jewish fast day falling on the tenth day of Tishri, the seventh month of the ecclesiastical year in the Jewish calendar, and following the Jewish new year (Rosh ha-Shanah). Yom Kippur is a day of personal repentance and of reconciliation with one's fellow human beings.

❖

Jewish Lives